NEW FRONTIERS IN HISTORY

series editors

Mark Greengrass
Department of History, Sheffield University

John Stevenson
Worcester College, Oxford

This important series reflects the substantial expansion that has occurred in the scope of history syllabuses. As new subject areas have emerged and syllabuses have come to focus more upon methods of historical enquiry and knowledge of source materials, a growing need has arisen for correspondingly broad-ranging textbooks.

New Frontiers in History provides up-to-date overviews of key topics in British, European and world history, together with accompanying source material and appendices. Authors focus on subjects where revisionist work is being undertaken, providing a fresh viewpoint, welcomed by students and sixth-formers. The series also explores established topics which have attracted much conflicting analysis and require a synthesis of the state of debate.

MANCHESTER
UNIVERSITY PRESS

The Stalin years
The Soviet Union 1929–1953

Evan Mawdsley

Manchester University Press

Manchester and New York

distributed exclusively in the USA by Palgrave

Published by Manchester University Press
Oxford Road, Manchester M13 9NR, UK
and Room 400, 175 Fifth Avenue, New York, NY 10010, USA

Distributed exclusively in the USA by
Palgrave, 175 Fifth Avenue, New York,
NY 10010, USA

Distributed exclusively in Canada by
UBC Press, University of British Colombia, 2029 West Mall,
Vancouver, BC, Canada V6T 1Z2

2 0 0 0 0 0 4 8 7 4

British Library Cataloguing-in-Publication Data
A catalogue record for this book is available from the British Library

Library of Congress Cataloging-in-Publication Data applied for

ISBN   0 7190 4599 1 *hardback*
        0 7190 4600 9 *paperback*

First published 1998

08 07 06 05 04 03 02 01   10 9 8 7 6 5 4 3 2

Typeset in Great Britain
by Helen Skelton, London
Printed in Great Britain
by Bell & Bain Ltd, Glasgow

Contents

Introduction

Explaining Stalinism

Joseph Stalin, born Iosif Vissarionovich Dzhugashvili, dominated an era in Russian history. By 1929 he had become the leading political figure in the USSR, effectively a dictator. He would hold this position until his death in 1953. The economy and society were transformed by the triple revolution of industrialisation, collectivisation and education which began with the 1st Five-year plan of 1928–32. In Stalin's second decade Russia became a great power again and played a decisive part in the Second World War – under Stalin as supreme commander-in-chief. By 1949 the USSR was a nuclear superpower, and Stalin the leader of a vast socialist bloc. All these achievements were paid for at a terrible cost.

There are a number of different ways of considering the Stalin period. First of all: how did twenty-four years of Stalinism fit into the seventy-four years of the Communist era in Russia? Were the developments under Stalin the logical consequence of the Bolshevik revolution and Lenin's understanding of Marxism? Or did they mark a fundamental discontinuity, a distortion or even a negation of that revolution and those ideas? Leon Trotsky, who from exile wrote of 'the revolution betrayed', was the father of this discontinuity school. Trotsky was bitterly condemned by later Soviet writers, but insofar as there was an official Soviet criticism of Stalin – after his death – it also saw Stalin as a break. Both Khrushchev and Gorbachev saw themselves as attempting to return to some kind of unspoilt Leninism of the October 1917 revolution, stressing the discontinuity of the Stalin years. And this raises the another aspect of discontinuity: whether Stalin's Communist successors were themselves able fundamentally to break away from his system.

For others, continuity rather than discontinuity has been a central feature of the Communist era. Many western historians and political scientists, especially in the Cold War era of the 1950s and 1960s, emphasised both the Leninist roots of Stalinism and the continuity of 'totalitarianism' after 1953. Paradoxically, for most of the post-Stalin period, excluding the Khrushchev and Gorbachev years, the official Soviet interpretation stressed continuity – of achievement – across the whole Communist era. This continuity school was perhaps reinforced by the collapse of Soviet Communism in the 1980s, when Stalin's legacy was seen as a continuing flaw in the system. There remains an even broader period of continuity to consider – that between Imperial Russia and Stalinist Russia – with some historians seeing 1917–29 as a short break in a long continuum of state–society relations.

A second, related, question is why did 'Stalinism' happen? To what extent was the development the result of Stalin's personality and choice, and to what extent was it the result of the situation within which he existed? This can be seen in terms also used to explain the Hitler years in Germany: 'intentionalist' and 'structuralist' – the dictator as the conscious maker of history, or the dictator as the product of deeper forces. These issues of periodisation and causation are linked. The structuralist view is closer to the continuity school, and the intentionalist closer to that of discontinuity.

Related to these in turn is a third question: what is the nature of the Soviet system? Whereas the Nazi era died with Hitler in 1945, the Soviet system survived Stalin's death, and unlike the Third Reich it was the subject of forty years' analysis by political scientists (i.e. from the late 1940s) as well as by historians; it was really from this that the idea of totalitarianism emerged. The best-known version of the totalitarian model stressed the features of absolute control in the system, a syndrome of certain symptoms. Totalitarianism is a concept used by the Italian Fascists to describe – positively – their own system, but it was used comparatively to link together Nazi Germany, Fascist Italy and Soviet Russia. Such a comparison seemed less convincing in the 1950s and 1960s than in the 1940s, partly as a result of a toning down of Cold War rhetoric, partly from a sense that Russia under Khrushchev (1955–64) and even under Brezhnev (1964–82) was different from Russia under Stalin, and partly from a scholarly consensus that the totalitarian model was both unrealistic and too static. In contrast there emerged among political scientists a 'conflict school'. This stressed debates behind the scenes, conflict based either on personal groupings (personalities and their followers) or on bureaucratic interests (the ideologists, the military, the industrialists, etc.). Although the conflict model was initially used to assess development in the contemporary USSR of the 1950s and 1960s, some historians also used it to try to understand the workings of Stalinist Russia.

A second non-totalitarian analysis, which came from the social sciences in the 1960s, was the developmental one. Influenced both by world-wide post-colonial change and by the technological achievements of the USSR (Sputnik and so on), this focused on economic modernisation. The attraction of this approach is that it caught the dynamism of the Stalin years – whatever the policies of the Stalin era were about they were not about the maintenance of the status quo. In addition the approach also captured the long-term consequences of the social and economic development which softened the Soviet system, and led to its eventual collapse.

Partly as a result of these new perspectives western historians began from the 1960s to re-examine the Stalinist past. Two aspects were most important. First, many of them now had, in common with historians looking at other countries and periods, a greater interest in society than in high politics. A new generation, products of the 1960s' expansion of the universities and post-graduate studies, saw both the Russian revolution and the years that followed it from a bottom-up rather than a top-down perspective. Even for those who concentrated on politics there was, as a result, a questioning of the totalitarian/intentionalist orthodoxy. Second, a separate school of revisionism in the 1960s and 1970s, concerned with Cold War international relations, questioned the orthodox view that Russia was solely responsible for the conflict.

The Stalin years, then, by the 1970s and early 1980s, were already an historical frontier, rich in argument. This was true despite limited access to sources. All the earlier approaches to the history of Stalinism – continuity/discontinuity, intentionalist/structuralist, totalitarian/conflict, orthodox/revisionist, developmental – had drawn on broadly similar source material, for the most part the Soviet press and other material published in the USSR. There was an occasional chink in the wall of secrecy, such as that provided by the writings of émigrés or local archives captured by the German army. More information had emerged in the relatively liberal time of Khrushchev, in particular his 'secret speech' of 1956, the mass of military memoirs, and even some specialised historical studies. After Khrushchev's fall in 1964 his cautious successors greatly limited the flow of official information, but avoided the extremities of Stalinist censorship and repression. Soviet citizens were told little about the recent past – except for the war – but in the west Khrushchev's own taped memoirs became available, as did the work of dissident historians like Roy Medvedev and the oral history of Solzhenitsyn. Later, in the détente period of the 1970s, a few western historians were able to gain access to some of the less secret Soviet archives dealing with the events of the 1917 revolution and the 1920s.

The real sea change, however, was Gorbachev's *glasnost* (openness) of the late 1980s. Hitherto secret documents from the Stalin years were published, and there was much greater access to the archives. In January 1989 the monthly *Izvestiia* (bulletin) of the Central Committee resumed publication; Khrushchev's secret speech appeared in full in one of the first issues, and a wealth of material followed on the Stalin period – especially on Stalinist terror. Both Khrushchev and Gorbachev had political motives for encouraging greater historical candour, but Gorbachev's historical agenda was longer than Khrushchev's. Khrushchev had 'rehabilitated' leaders purged by Stalin, but Gorbachev went further back; most strikingly he rehabilitated Bukharin, the 'rightist' leader of the 1920s, whose policies had much in common with his own. Gorbachev encouraged a campaign to fill in the blank pages of Soviet history. After the collapse of the USSR in 1991 the area of criticism became even broader and general attacks on Communism (and Leninism) and not just on the excesses of

Stalin or Brezhnev, became possible: indeed, in Yeltsin's Russia, they became politically correct. On top of this the partial opening of the archives set off something of a gold rush of western research, continuing throughout the 1990s.

If the western historical debate and the opening of the archives were not enough there was a third development which would transform the way in which historians dealt with the Stalin years: the collapse of the USSR itself. It finally occurred in December 1991 but had been on the cards since Brezhnev's death in 1982. By the 1980s it was clear that, leaving aside issues of morality, there was something unviable about the Soviet system. The colossus, it was increasingly pointed out, had feet of clay. The economy turned out to be in an even worse state than pessimistic western economic analysts had estimated. The impact of totalitarian indoctrination was more superficial than had been alleged. The power of national sentiment among ethnic minorities and the power of Russian nationalism were both surprising features of the final crisis. And whatever the causes of the collapse, it was now possible to look back on the complete Soviet experience, and to assess Stalin's place within this whole.

Marxist theory and Bolshevik practice

Some respected historians hold that neither Stalin nor the Stalinist elite took ideology seriously and that the mass of party members simply did not understand it; ideology is thus not a serious element of the explanation of Stalinism. My interpretation goes in the opposite direction: it is impossible to understand the actions and attitudes of Stalin and the ruling party without paying serious attention to Marxism-Leninism.

'Leninism', Stalin declared, 'is Marxism of the era of imperialism and the proletarian revolution.'[1] Lenin grafted on top of the thought of Marx and Engels notions of his own about the role of the revolutionary party and imperialism. Stalin added little to Marxism-Leninism. The idea of 'Stalinism' as a separate ideology was never really taken up, and Stalin consistently based his ideas on Lenin's thought. The validity of Marxism-Leninism seemed to be confirmed for the first two generations of Soviet leaders by the events through which they lived, and this was reinforced by formal and informal political education. The

Communist party's official programme throughout Stalin's period in power was one drafted in 1919, which replaced a pre-revolutionary programme of 1903 and would not itself be replaced
until 1961. Stalin derived much of his own early prestige from
his role as a systematiser of Marxism-Leninism, especially in his
1924 pamphlet, *Foundations of Leninism*. Another central text
would be the 1938 *History of the Communist Party of the Soviet
Union (Short Course)*, which was both a (very biased) history of
the party and a codification of its ideas.

So, what were the key points of this ideology, as understood by
Marx, Lenin and Stalin? First of all, a central place was occupied
by the urban working class, rather than any other class or national group. The rise of Marxism in Russia followed the growth of
the urban working class in the 1890s, and Marxism stressed the
dynamic force of the urban proletariat; the nineteenth century
European movement – in Germany and elsewhere – was also
built around workers. Although a number of the Russian
Marxist leaders – like Lenin and, arguably, Stalin – were members of the intelligentsia, there was also a substantial plebeian
element both in the underground party and in the mass party,
which ballooned out during the revolution and civil war. The
Communists were quite capable of suppressing the urban working class; they did so on numerous occasions, especially during
the civil war. But that did not change their overall orientation.
The relatively greater resistance of the rural peasantry to early
Communist policies confirmed to the regime that the urban
working class was its best base of support, and that it alienated
them at its peril. The basic problem, however, was that this con-
stituency made up only a small part of the Russian population.

In Marxist ideology, and in Russian historical practice, the
favoured class operated within a world of struggle. Violent class
struggle was the motor of history and for Russian Marxists the
implications, both internally and internationally, were severe. It
is true that by the end of the nineteenth century a changing situation in western and central Europe suggested, at least to some
Marxists there, that peaceful reform was an alternative road to
the betterment of the working class's condition. This was, however, emphatically rejected by the Russian Marxists and especially by the Leninist hard-liners. Indeed the nature of Russian
society and the power and inflexibility of the old Tsarist state

made the whole local political tradition one which stressed revolutionary rather than parliamentary activity; this was true both for the Marxists and for the peasant-based socialists who preceded and paralleled them.

This centrality of the class struggle seemed to be confirmed by the history of three Russian revolutions (one in 1905 and two in 1917) and of the civil war. This last event, which took place from 1917–20, pitted the Russian working class against all other elements of the Russian population and indeed against the whole outside world, portrayed as the forces of international imperialism. It was important as an intense formative experience for hundreds of thousands of party members who were brought to political activity during it and who inherited power as a result of it. The civil war – coupled with the experience of the First World War – also led to a militarisation of the Communist movement and its ideology. Constant class struggle made compromise difficult or impossible; it was not only Stalin who saw enemies everywhere, and it was not a mentality confined to the 1930s. The young Dzhugashvili-Stalin was attractive to Lenin in 1912 mainly because he was such an adherent of struggle, an agent, participant and victim of class warfare, and such an opponent of compromise. Dzhugashvili saw himself in precisely that way, which is why he adopted a name based on the Russian word for 'steel' (*stal'*); his future lieutenant, Viacheslav Skriabin, would take the pseudonym 'Molotov' from 'hammer' (*molot*) for the same reason. Stalin did eventually accentuate this aspect of the ideology, especially from 1928 onwards in his frequent remarks about the intensification of the class struggle as the proletariat moved closer to victory (see document 3).

Another aspect of the focus on class and class struggle was that the ideology was effectively non-rural, or even anti-rural. Marx had had little time for the peasants, regarding them as a class that belonged to the past. It is true that Lenin devoted more attention both in theory and practice to the peasantry, and that in the debates of the mid-1920s Trotsky would be accused by the Stalinists of under-estimating the revolutionary potential of the peasantry (see document 1). The Bolsheviks had made an important compromise to their ideals with the decree of November 1917 which transferred the land of the big landowners not to socialist farms but to individual peasant households. The civil war, with its crises of food requisitioning and army recruitment, even with rural revolt, intensified the Communist party's distrust of the peasantry. This is not to say that its leaders were ignorant of peasant life. Many 'worker' Communists, both in the party leadership and the urban rank and file, had grown up in the countryside and kept links with it and, if anything, that proportion increased with the mass migrations, the 'ruralisation' of the cities, in the early Stalin years. But these migrants did not see village life as an ideal. The party also employed a crude sociology of the peasantry. The Marxist urban perspective was one in which it was hard to find a place for the peasants, and they were treated as the 'petty bourgeoisie'. There was an attempt to single out the better off peasants – the *kulaks* – as particular enemies of the urban proletariat and the poor peasants as potential allies, but there remained a distrust of the villages that was potentially very ominous. On the one hand the peasants made up the overwhelming mass of the Russian population, and on the other the status quo in the countryside was seen as unviable.

The ideology of class struggle led to a particular notion of government, that of a dictatorship not of an individual but of a class. Marx's dictatorship of the proletariat was defined in the Russian Communist party's 1919 programme as 'the conquest by the proletariat of such a degree of political power as will enable it to crush the resistance of the exploiters'. It was partly as a result of rigid adherence to that concept by Lenin that power-sharing with other socialist parties was rejected in November 1917 and later. In practical terms it assigned the leading role, both in the seizure of power and the subsequent dictatorship, to a party of professional revolutionaries. Lenin had stressed the vanguard party in his pamphlet *What is to be Done?* of 1902 and this was indeed one of the core notions of Leninism. It was born out of the struggle for power under the conditions of the Tsarist autocracy, but the backbone role of the party developed further in the civil war. The Communist party itself was run under Lenin's principles of 'democratic centralism' (the noun was more important than the adjective), and this was confirmed by the 1921 ban on factions within the party. As far as outsiders were concerned there was an emphasis on the infallibility of the party. What emerged was an essentially top-down relationship between the party and the mass of society. Party guidance of the new Soviet state was formalised at the 8th party congress in 1919. The mechanical metaphor of transforming all non-party organisations into 'transmission belts', linking the party and the working class, was a doctrine of the Stalinists as a party in power. But it was the institutionalisation of principles laid out by Lenin twenty years previously. In later years central control would be extended from within the boundaries of Russia to the 'Bolshevisation' of the Communist International (the Comintern), and then to the assertion of strict control over new socialist governments in other countries.

The economic side of Marxist revolutionary ideology centred on the inner contradictions of capitalism and the inevitability of its collapse. For the Russian Bolsheviks as a revolutionary Marxist party in power this had weighty implications. Although they compromised in a number of ways during the civil war – for example in their treatment of the peasants, of the nationalities, even of the church – they were throughout bitterly antagonistic to a market economy. The set of radical economic policies known later as 'War Communism' involved attempts at centralisation and state control, and they became official doctrine from October 1917. The New Economic Policy (NEP) of 1921, the partial restoration of the market in agricultural produce, was forced on Lenin and his comrades by an intense crisis. Economic preconceptions – especially the imminence of the collapse of capitalism on a world scale – would also dominate the Communists' view of the outside world.

There were other ways in which Marxist-Leninist notions of the class struggle carried over into a highly ideologised policy both towards the national minorities of the Russian Empire and towards states outside the old empire. Marxism was internationalist: 'Workers of the world unite, you have nothing to lose but your chains!' Marx and Engels had had little time for the aspirations of the national minorities, which were seen to run at cross purposes to the struggle between classes and to be the aspirations only of the national bourgeoisie. The Russian Communist leaders, even had they not stressed other reasons for the importance of dictatorship and centralisation, would have been intolerant of the claims for 'dis-union' from the national minorities – despite the fact that many of the first generation of Communist leaders came from such groups. And as for relations with other states, the accepted perception – based more on Lenin than Marx – was that conflict with and within the capitalist world was unavoidable. This theoretical view seemed to be confirmed by the experience of the civil war, when Russia faced the hostility of the outside world.

The famous conflict between Stalin and Trotsky in the 1920s about Russia's place in this international scheme of things also needs to be seen as much from the point of view of ideology as personality. 'Socialism in one country', the notion that Russia in isolation could make great progress towards building socialism (see document 1), was a Stalinist principle not incompatible with late Leninism. Only a few days after the critically ill Lenin made a personal condemnation of Stalin in his December 1922 'Testament' he wrote a valedictory note, 'Our Revolution', endorsing revolution from above and, by implication, the possibility of building socialism in an isolated backward country. Socialism in one country may not have been great Marxism, but neither was it simply Stalinism: it owed much to Lenin, and probably reflected the opinion of the mass of party members. Socialism in one country also did not rule out a great interest in developing – and controlling – the revolutionary movement in the outside world.

Iosif Dzhugashvili-Stalin

Ideology and early revolutionary experience provide part of the background for what happened between 1929 and 1953, but another part is the key individual. Stalin is sometimes reduced to a representative of the bureaucracy, a mediocrity, others have attempted to explain the Stalin years on the basis of the personality of this extraordinary man.

The future *vozhd'* (leader) was born in the small town of Gori in Georgia. His official date of birth was later to be 9 December 1879, in the twenty-fourth year of the reign of Emperor Alexander II.[2] He died, evidently as the result of a brain haemorrhage, in March 1953; he was seventy-three and had been in poor health for two or three years. The son of a shoemaker, whatever his abilities Stalin could never, even had he been born only a quarter of a century earlier, have aspired to be more than a village priest. The fact that he was a *gruzin* (Georgian) was signifi-

Introduction

cant; much has been made of Stalin the 'Asiatic', but in the opposite sense it was remarkable that a member of one of the national minorities should have become a statesman associated with
Russian power, Russian nationalism and tight state centralisation. There were only 1.4 million Georgians out of the Russian
Empire's 1897 population of 125.7 million, they were Christians
– having converted five centuries before the Slavs (and
Dzhugashvili's mother was devout) – and they spoke a language
completely different from Russian. But the epoch of 1917 was a
peculiar window of opportunity for members of the minorities.
Neither in the Russian Empire nor the mature Soviet Union did
non-Russians have much chance to reach the supreme level of
independent political-bureaucratic leadership. The Bolshevik
party of the period before and during the revolution, however,
had a leadership of outsiders, with a high non-Russian element.

Dzhugashvili was an outstanding pupil in the Church primary school in Gori, and then moved on to one of the main educational centres of the Transcaucasus, the Orthodox Seminary at
Tiflis (Tbilisi), which he entered in 1894. He was then fourteen,
and before his expulsion five years later he received a useful general education, although the Tiflis seminary was not, to be sure,
of the standard of St Petersburg or Moscow University.
However, compared with the average (male) inhabitant of the
Russian empire – who would be fortunate to get a few years of
village school before beginning work in field or factory –
Dzhugashvili's education was impressive.

Like a number of other young men of his generation, living on
the margins of this modernising society, Stalin was drawn to
Marxism. The revolutionary struggle hardened him, as it did
many others. For sixteen years of young adulthood and early
middle age (1901–17) he lived as an 'illegal' or in some remote
place of 'internal exile'. He was arrested in 1902, 1908 and in
early 1913, and subsequently sentenced to long periods of exile.
It is hardly surprising that he – and his generation of party leaders – took conspiracy and the class struggle so seriously.

Stalin was also a man of a limited personal experience. When
he flew to meet Churchill and Roosevelt at the Teheran
Conference in 1943 he was making his first trip outside the
Russian Empire for thirty years. He had made a few previous
brief trips abroad – to party meetings in Stockholm, London and

11

Cracow – but his longest trip had been in 1912–13, when he spent a few months in Cracow and Vienna. A particularly formative experience for this middle-aged, inexperienced man – and for a generation of revolutionaries – was the 1919–20 civil war. When it began he was a nonentity, except within a tiny radical party, and the best years of his life were seemingly over. When it ended he was one of the top half-dozen leaders of the largest country on earth. In between, the struggle for survival left a very deep imprint on his approach, his appreciation of the value of force to overcome opponents, and even on his discourse.

Stalin's personal life reinforces the one-dimensional nature of the man. The only surviving child, he lost contact with his father, who apparently died in poverty in 1909. His mother survived for thirty more years, but in adulthood Stalin saw her on only a handful of occasions. He married twice, in 1906 and 1918. His first wife, Ekaterina Svanidze, died of typhus a year after a church wedding; his second, Nadezhda Allilueva, shot herself in 1932. Allilueva was only sixteen at the time of her wedding – half Stalin's age – and her fourteen years of marriage were difficult. After her death Stalin had remote relationships with his two sons, and a difficult one with his daughter. Yakov (Svanidze's son) killed himself in German captivity; Vasilii, born to Stalin and Allilueva in 1921, climbed to dizzy heights in the Soviet air force only to drink himself to death in 1962; Svetlana Allilueva, born in 1926, had a troubled life and left the only personal account of the dysfunctional family.[3]

Stalin's was an extraordinary personality, and much effort has been spent in trying to understand it. He was not a populist, not a great speaker, not an original thinker. But if he was not the 'towering genius of humanity' that the propaganda of his later life would have it, he was highly intelligent. He had a prodigious memory, a mastery of detail, and he was a very hard worker. (We have remarkable disinterested witnesses to this in the form of the western statesmen and generals who dealt with him at wartime conference.) Stalin is often compared with his contemporaries Hitler and Mussolini, but the differences are highly significant. Hitler and Mussolini had come to power as charismatic leaders of mass movements, and once in power proved to be indifferent administrators. Although Stalin had played an active part in the revolutionary underground, and in the events of 1917 and the civil war, he was a second generation supreme leader who had inherited Lenin's mantle through political infighting. It was what he was exceptionally good at, and he turned out to be a man whose political strategy was both cunning and long-sighted.[4] That is not to say that he was truly efficient, or that he was all-knowing, however, and his actions were warped by a highly suspicious nature. What Stalin did have in common with Hitler and Mussolini was that he identified himself with the central idea of the movement. He was in some material senses not self-indulgent, but in his self-identification with Lenin and revolution he was incredibly vain.

******

All this, then, is the starting point for a study of the Stalin years themselves. Above all this book is an attempt to see the Stalin era as a whole. As much attention is paid to the 1940s and early 1950s as to the 1930s and late 1920s – taking in both wooden ploughs and the atomic bomb. With this in mind the book has been organised into thematic chapters, each of which looks at the twenty-five years of Stalinism as a whole. Because the book is organised in this way it is important to bear in mind the connections between themes, especially the link between foreign policy and domestic policy. Chapter 1 discusses the political system within which Stalin came to power, and also provides a narrative framework for the whole period. The extraordinary economic developments – industrialisation, collectivisation, war mobilisation, post-war reconstruction, the flourishing of the 'command-administrative system' – are the subject of Chapter 2. The impact of those changes on Russian society, and the impact of Russian society on the system, are discussed in Chapter 3. Chapter 4 deals with the related development – and supervision – of a new form of culture. After the events of 1989–91 it is impossible to discuss Soviet history without considering that half of the population who were not ethnic Russians; the nationalities under Stalin form the basis of Chapter 5. Chapter 6 examines the nature of Soviet foreign and military policy, before, during, and after the Second World War and, finally, Chapter 7 turns to the most extraordinary and controversial aspect of the Stalin years: the system of terror directed both at the general population and at the elite.

Notes

1 I. V. Stalin, *Voprosy leninizma* (Moscow, 1945), p. 2

2 Edvard Radzinsky found archival evidence that Stalin was actually born a year earlier, in December 1878: E. Radzinsky, *Stalin* (London, 1996), pp. 11–14; see also *Izvestiia TsK*, 1990, no. 7, p. 124. Although this detail is in itself unimportant it exemplifies the mystery which surrounded Stalin's life and career from the very beginning; there are other mysteries about his death.

3 Svetlana Allilueva, *20 Letters to a Friend* (London, 1967).

4 This emerges particularly in his candid correspondence with Molotov in the 1920s and 1930s. See L. Lih *et al.*, *Stalin's Letters to Molotov, 1925–1936* (New Haven, 1995).

1

The dictatorship of the proletariat: Stalinism and politics

One of Stalin's few post-war public speeches was given in the Moscow's Bolshoi Theatre in February 1946 (see document 15). The Leader was standing for re-election as a Supreme Soviet deputy and was addressing the voters of the capital's Stalinskii borough. Stalin's speech did not influence the outcome – he was the only candidate – but his words were significant as an extended self-justification. As far as the state was concerned, Stalin argued, the Second World War swept aside the claims of the foreign press. The 'Soviet social system' was not a '"risky experiment", doomed to failure' or a 'rootless, house of cards imposed on the people by the organs of the *Cheka* [the secret police]. The war has shown that the Soviet social system is a genuinely popular system [and] a fully viable and sturdy form of government'.[1]

The party-state regime

The term 'regime' will be used here to describe that form of government, despite its negative Cold War connotations ('we have *governments*, they have *regimes*'), as to talk simply about the 'government' or the 'state' would be to omit the leading role of the Communist party. This party-state regime was not specifically Stalinist, but endured throughout the era of Communist rule in Russia, from the winter of 1917–18 to 1991. The Supreme Soviet, to which Stalin was re-elected as a deputy in 1946 was a sham parliament, meeting for only a few days a year, but it should not be dismissed out of hand. In the mid-1930s 98 per cent of the total population were not members of the Communist party, and it was important to have a 'transmission belt' from the party to the non-party element. Real political power, however, was to be found elsewhere in the system, in what might be called the executive branch of the state and the party. Lenin's most important political day-to-day power came from being 'state' prime minister, chairman of the cabinet. This body was originally called the Council of People's Commissars (*Sovnarkom*), but in 1946 was renamed the Council of Ministers. Stalin, in contrast, did not become prime minister until May 1941, a dozen years after he became the pre-eminent leader. That does not mean, however, that the state executive institutions were unimportant until then. Rykov, Lenin's successor, was a powerful figure as prime minister from 1924 to 1930 and Molotov, prime minister from 1930 to 1941, was second only to Stalin. The power of the state was, however, effectively increased from 1941 when Stalin combined in his person the party and state hierarchies. When Stalin's successors modified the system they tried, spasmodically, to prohibit this combination and to keep the same individual from being both head of the party and prime minister. In fact, however, the party-state link had been the source of Stalin's *later* absolute power rather than the cause of his rise to prominence. The ministers (people's commissars up to 1946) were key actors in the system, although the shape and role of *Sovnarkom* changed drastically in the 1930s, expanding from about a dozen conventional government departments (foreign affairs, interior, war, etc.) to a system of over fifty, the majority charged with running one or another branch of the socialist economy. This system would continue to the end of the Soviet period, with only one break during the Khrushchev years.

The other side of this dual system was the party. It was Stalin who perfected what hostile writers called the 'partocracy' (*partokratiia*), but much of this was already in place in Lenin's lifetime: of course, the Communist (Bolshevik) party preceded the Soviet state, and the logic of the ideology was that the party was the basis of the dictatorship of the proletariat. From 1917 the party, for all its inefficiencies, provided a supporting mesh to the state based on reliability and personal contacts. From 1919 party groups were instructed to dominate the local state organisations, and even at the centre strategic political decisions were made in party organisations rather than state ones, even though after the spring of 1918 there were no non-Communists in *Sovnarkom*.

Party power was concentrated in the top layers of the party, despite the democratic principles laid out in various versions of its official rules. Local party organisations elected – directly or indirectly – delegates to party congresses, which met for week or less, at intervals of a year or more. They confirmed basic political decisions – the political 'line' – and they elected standing organisations to oversee the party's activities until the next congress. By far the most important of these standing organisations was the Central Committee. This body met in plenary sessions (plenums) at shorter and shorter intervals – by the 1920s typically two or three times a year and for three or four days at a time. From 1919 the day-to-day functions of the Central Committee had formally been taken over by sub-committees, of which the most important in the long term was the political bureau, or Politburo. The Politburo (Presidium after 1952) was a group of about fifteen voting and non-voting members, and met weekly.

The reality was even less democratic and stable. First of all, there was a tendency – going back to the immediate post-revolutionary period – for party institutions to meet less frequently. There were annual party congresses until 1925, then larger and larger gaps between them, with meetings in 1927, 1930, 1934 and 1939. The 1939 congress was followed by an extraordinary gap of thirteen years before the 19th Congress in 1952. The Central Committee grew larger and larger, from 46 voting and non-voting (candidate) members in 1922 to 236 in 1952. It became more representative of the elite but lost in the process a sense of political cohesion. In the later Soviet years, plenums of the Central Committee were held less frequently than in the early Soviet period, only three times between 1941 and 1952. The Politburo, the Central Committee sub-committee, maintained a fairly constant size but from the late 1930s it met less frequently as a unified body, being replaced by commissions or sub-committees. Some of these developments, at least in their extreme form, were uniquely Stalinist, as the party's rules for running its affairs were arbitrarily ignored by its leader. More accurately, however, they were 'late Stalinist'. In the 1920s and 1930s Stalin had used party congresses and plenums to build and consolidate his power:

there were three congresses and two conferences between 1929 and 1941. In contrast – and in violation of the 1939 party rules – there were after the Second World War no congresses, very few Central Committee plenums and, after 1946, even the Politburo met very seldom as a unified body. It was essentially this that Khrushchev and the party oligarchy condemned in the 'party revival' of the 1950s. The party certainly operated more constitutionally from 1952, at least in terms of frequency of congresses and plenums. On the other hand the control of the party central organs by a leading group (not to mention the party's dictatorship over society) was something that had existed from the very beginning and would continue to the 1980s.

The top elite of the party, centred first on Lenin, then on a group of potential successors and finally on Stalin, was able to maintain itself in power from above. The ruling group or individual ruler decided in advance who would be 'elected' to the Central Committee. In addition, posts throughout the system, in the party and the state, centrally as well as locally, were filled by individuals approved formally by the ruling group. These 'reliable' office holders made up the delegations to party congresses and, at the top level, membership of the Central Committee. In what western political scientists have called 'the circular flow of power' they in turn 'elected' the leadership. The growing power of central appointment also led to the development of the *nomenklatura* system. This Russian word can be translated as 'list'. One specific meaning for this system was a list of posts (more accurately a set of different lists) in the party and state (and army, etc.) to which new appointments had to be approved by specific party bodies or, more exactly, by permanent officials within them; a secondary meaning of *nomenklatura* is the party-based elite as a whole. This system to some extent antedated Stalin's domination of Soviet politics; in fact it brought him to power and it would continue long after his death.

Especially important within this top-down reality was the secretariat of the Central Committee, which was the essence of the apparatus (*apparat*), the machinery of party administration. Here, most famously, was one key to Stalin's rise to power. In April 1922 he was made general secretary of the Central Committee. Up to that time, although a party leader, a specialist on the nationalities and a major trouble-shooter, Stalin's posts were not in the very first rank – he was commissar for nationalities and head of the inspectorate (*rabkrin*). However, as general secretary he developed extensive powers of positive and negative patronage, with the help of other party secretaries elected from the Central Committee membership, the most powerful of whom were the youthful Viacheslav Molotov and Lazar' Kaganovich (see document 19). Under Stalin, too, the secretariat was elaborated into a system of departments (*otdely*) and subdepartments. The party – rather than the state – machinery also became the focus of power in the localities, something which would further enhance his power but which would also endure for thirty-eight years after his death.

The Stalin era was not just about the rise of one man. If it had been, the political system would have changed more in 1953 when that one man died. The Stalin years were also about the rise and fall of elite generations. Stalin came to power within an elite thrown up by the revolution. They were comrades who had been at least rank-and-file members of the pre-revolutionary underground party, and who were still in early middle age in the late 1920s and early 1930s. The majority of this revolutionary generation supported Stalin directly or indirectly in the political power struggle of the 1920s, and even more supported his general line of rapid industrialisation and comprehensive collectivisation. They shared his analysis of society, and his two-camps view of the outside world (see p. 80). They were the 'victors' of the 1934 'congress of the victors'. They were, as they described themselves at the time, 'Stalinists'. A few dozen of them – such as Molotov, Kaganovich, Voroshilov and Andreev – formed a close-knit Stalin team (*Komanda*) and would remain in power for a long time, even after his death. Even so, many – but not all – of the revolutionary generation were destroyed in the purges of 1937–38; why that should be so is considered in Chapter 7.

These early Stalinists were largely replaced as a political elite, either after 1937 or in the following decade or so, by another leadership generation, which was also Stalinist, but in a different way. The early Stalinists had supported Stalin in the political debates and economic experiments of the 1920s; the late Stalinists were a product of those experiments. They were young; ethnic Russians formed a higher proportion, which contributed to a more nationalistic outlook; they were on the whole from the masses, especially from the village-born workers; they were the products of the social revolutions of 1917–20 and 1928–32. They had a range of experiences, but practical contributions to the economy were seen as important, and many of those who rose to the top were trained as engineers. More than those in the revolutionary generation they were careerists. They were perhaps less independently minded *vis à vis* Stalin, and they were less critical due to their acceptance of successes. But they were not simply creatures of Stalin, and had interests of their own. They would live on well after his death, and some have even since called these late Stalinists the 'Brezhnev generation' (see document 19).

The final aspect of party-state regime involves a lower level of politically privileged people, the Communist party's membership (see Table 1.1). In the post-Stalin period, and especially from the Khrushchev years onwards, being a party member was not very unusual, indeed it was the prerequisite for career advancement. By the 1980s 19 million people, about 7 per cent of the total population (688 in 10,000, perhaps 15 per cent of the adult population), were party members or candidates (probationary members). Great changes occurred in the level of party saturation over the Stalin years. On the eve of February 1917 active party membership had been tiny. The usually cited total of 24,000 was probably an exaggeration but, even if correct, as a ratio of the total Russian population it meant something like 2 in every 10,000 people. It was from within that pool of 24,000 underground veterans that most of the national leadership would be drawn for the next twenty years, to 1937. Throughout the period of Stalin's rise the Communist party was in a very exposed position. At the height of the NEP in 1926, even after nearly a decade in power, Communist party members and candidates numbered only about 1 million, less than 1 per cent of the total population (73 people in 10,000), or perhaps 2 per cent of the working population. The revolutionary period of the 1st Five-year plan (1927–32) trebled the size of the party, but still to only about two per cent of the total population. After the mass influx there was no recruiting for five years and, from late 1932, there was a mass clear-out, as unsatisfactory people were 'purged', i.e., in this case, expelled from the party. This, together with another kind of purge, the bloody one of 1937–38, hit the party membership hard. On the other hand the gates to party entry opened again in 1939 and were kept open during the war and, significantly, in the post-war years. Communists (including 'candidate' members) rose to about 3.5 per cent of the total population (345 in 10,000) by the eve of Stalin's death; perhaps 7 per cent of the working population, and a substantially higher proportion of the male urban population. This growth is historically interesting in two respects. First of all, it cuts across the commonly accepted notion that the party atrophied in Stalin's last decade, and second it can be seen as indicative of the greater sense of security of the regime, a sense that may have been shared by Stalin.

Table 1.1   *Communist party membership*

Year	Full members	Candidates	Total	Total population
1917 (1913)	24,000	–	24,000	159,200,000
1924	350,000	122,000	472,000	
1926	639,652	440,162	1,079,814	147,000,000
1933	2,203,951	1,351,387	3,555,338	
1939	1,514,181	792,792	2,306,973	194,000,000
1945	3,965,530	1,794,839	5,760,369	
1953	6,067,027	830,197	6,897,224	
1970	13,810,089	645,232	14,455,321	241,700,000
1986	18,288,786	715,592	19,004,378	276,300,000

Note: Membership figures refer to 1 January of the given year.

The succession struggle and after

One of the most pondered questions of Soviet political history is why it was Stalin who came to supreme power at the end of the 1920s. He did it through the political framework just discussed, particularly through the Central Committee, the Secretariat and the Politburo. The power struggle during the 1920s was played out in a way which had much in common with Lenin's manoeuvrings for influence within the pre-revolutionary Marxist party, and also with the ways that Khrushchev, Brezhnev and even Gorbachev would consolidate power in their time. Lenin was incapacitated at the start of 1923, at which time the other voting members of the Politburo were Kamenev (1883–1936), Rykov

(1881–1938), Stalin (1878/9–1953), Tomskii (1880–1936), Trotsky (1879–1940) and Zinoviev (1883–1936); Bukharin (1888–1938), Kalinin (1875–1946), and Molotov (1890–1986) were non-voting candidate members. By the end of 1930 only Stalin, Molotov (his closest ally and subordinate), and Kalinin (a figurehead) were left. This transition happened in stages. A *troika* (triumvirate) formed within the Politburo to oppose Trotsky; Stalin allied with Grigorii Zinoviev and Lev Kamenev, both close comrades of Lenin's in the underground Bolshevik party. This was as much about personalities as about issues. Trotsky was removed from his power base, the war commissariat, in 1925. Within a short period the *troika* broke up. The dominant force in the Politburo became Stalin and Bukharin, with a programme built around support for the NEP. Their rivals became a so-called 'left' opposition which advocated, among other things, more rapid economic change. By the the end of 1925 Zinoviev had lost his power base in Leningrad, and in the following year in the Comintern. At the end of 1926 Zinoviev and then Trotsky were removed from the Politburo, and in the late autumn of 1927 they were both removed from the Central Committee, and then from the Communist party altogether. Trotsky refused to recant in his 'opposition' and was eventually exiled, first to Central Asia and then to the outer darkness beyond the Soviet border. The second round was fought out in the last three years of the 1920s. Stalin broke with Bukharin. The focus was again largely personalities, but also at issue were the beginnings of industrialisation and a growing confrontation with the country's peasant majority. Only three of the nine voting members of the Politburo were openly critical of the way things were going, however, and the 'right' opposition were gradually edged out of their posts: Tomskii from the trade unions, Bukharin from the Comintern and the party newspaper *Pravda*, and Rykov from the post of prime minister.

It was at the time of the defeat of the 'right' opposition that the propaganda organs started to emphasise Stalin as an individual. Much was made of Stalin's (supposed) fiftieth birthday in December 1929, although it was in the aftermath of the 1st Five-year plan, in 1932–33, that the full-blown 'cult of personality' appeared. By the end of the 1920s most of Stalin's party contemporaries, the men who had been leaders of the tiny pre-1917

Leninist party, had been removed from the top leadership. With Rykov's removal in December 1930 the Politburo consisted of Stalin and nine other voting members. These men were nearly all five to ten years younger than Stalin, and although they were veterans of the pre-revolutionary party they had served only in the rank and file. They lacked the prestige which came from having worked closely with Lenin, or even having served the amount of prison time that Stalin had. The enlarged party Central Committee – the elite of the Soviet system – now comprised people who had either never opposed Stalin or who had come back into favour when the general line shifted to the left. They accepted Stalin's leadership, and they supported his programmes of rapid industrialisation and collectivisation. But all this, and the apparent disappearance of factions, should not be taken to mean that elite politics had ceased. Historians debate the extent to which Stalin was challenged in the early 1930s as a result of the social chaos caused by the 1st Five-year plan, if not by members of the Politburo then by the 'barons' of the party Central Committee.[2] What is clear is that there were internal political conflicts between Stalin's lieutenants which belie the notion of a bureaucratic monolith.

What happened next, the purges, is dealt with in Chapter 7, and is best analysed after looking at all the pressures at work – economic, social, cultural, ethnic, international. For the moment it is enough to note that the terror of 1937–38 wiped out half to three-quarters of the top Stalinist leadership. The ruling group around Stalin – the 'Stalin team' (*Stalinskaia komanda*) – mostly survived unscathed. Of the ten voting members of the Politburo elected in 1934 only one was a direct purge victim; some of the others remained the power in the land until 1957. What they had in common was close personal contact with Stalin. He trusted them, insofar as he trusted anybody. The successes and excesses of the 1930s and 1940s was partly their responsibility. One group of Stalin's lieutenants were veterans from the revolutionary period who had sided with Stalin thoughout the debates of the 1920s. Molotov, Voroshilov (1881–1969) and Kalinin were the most senior, and Molotov had much the most political weight. A second group had a different kind of contact with Stalin. They were clever, hard-working and reliable young men from the *apparat* who were elevated to important positions by the talent-spotting general secretary. The best known of these – mainly because he was prime minister in 1953–55 – was Georgii Malenkov (1901–1988). Malenkov was sixteen at the time of the revolution and only joined the party three years later; he was advanced rapidly to take over a key department of the secretariat in 1934. From a similar background in the *apparat* came Nikolai Ezhov (1895–1940), who was a key *apparatchik* before being moved to the secret police (the NKVD) from 1936–38. The Georgian Lavrentii Beria (1899–1953) had an ethnic tie to Stalin, but was a former secret policeman – and later the first party secretary in Transcaucasia – brought in to replace Ezhov as head of the NKVD. Andrei Zhdanov (1896–1948) was another post-civil war regional leader brought into the secretariat and then rapidly advanced. Other younger members of the team advanced in the 1930s and early 1940s were Khrushchev (1895–1971), N. A. Voznesenskii (1903–50), and A. A. Kuznetsov (1905–50).

The war years seem almost to lack a political dimension. In contrast to the civil war period there were no party congresses or conferences during the Great Fatherland War and only one Central Committee plenum. One line of interpretation would be that it was precisely this lack of politics that helped the regime endure the defeats of 1941–42 without a high-level challenge (see document 12). There was politics of a sort in the final period, 1946 to 1953, which was almost as long as Khrushchev's years in supreme power (1957–64). By this time Stalin was an old man – his 70th birthday was extravagantly celebrated in 1949 – and the nature of Stalinist politics changed. Although some leaders were arrested the mass purge process was not in fact repeated, and most of the political elite enjoyed physical security (see Chapter 7). We have seen how the party constitution had been often ignored, and the final calling of the 19th party congress in October 1952 was probably a sign that the individuals who would dominate the leadership from 1953 to 1957 were already in a strong position. Stalin's physical powers were failing, after the exhausting life of sixteen-hour days and heavy smoking. He may have withdrawn from at least a part of his activities – this was certainly the case by 1951–52.[3] A spurt of activity at the very end of his life – a semi-public personal attack on Politburo members Molotov and Mikoian, the so-called Doctors' Plot – can be interpreted as a final effort to take control of the party or – and not altogether in contradiction – as a sign that Stalin was already a spent force.

*****

As Stalin told his electors in 1946, the Soviet system was indeed no 'house of cards'. The system had extraordinary strengths. There was also much continuity in Soviet politics. The Stalinist political system inherited many of its fundamentals from Leninism. Where Stalin introduced innovations or important modifications, they often continued under his successors. Examples were the *apparat*, the *nomenklatura*, mass party membership, the more developed state, large party bodies, the directly elected Supreme Soviet; indeed both Khrushchev and Gorbachev found what they inherited to be impossible to reform. Another continuity was the political conflict among secondary leaders and different interest groups, a feature from 1917 to 1991, including the period 1929–53. The political uniqueness of the Stalin years – aspects not repeated later and overtly rejected by successors – were the extravagance of the leader cult, the extent of the leader's personal power (over both party and state), his twenty-four years' tenure, the freedom of action given to extraordinary non-party organs (above all the secret police) and, connected with this, the use of extreme punishments. Even some of these extraordinary features, however, had been confined to short periods of Stalin's time in power.

Stalinist politics demonstrate some of the shortcomings of a simple totalitarian model. There were political conflicts that need to be taken into account, and like other political systems, the Stalinist regime did not exist in a vacuum; it evolved, and that evolution was a product of a changing society and external pressures. Political systems are also about ideas and outcomes, and one shortcoming of the totalitarian model is that it focuses so much on structures of control. The Stalinist party-state regime was not used to keep static control for an individual or even for an oligarchy. It forced extraordinary policies of economic and social mobilisation on society. The political system as it had evolved by 1929 had already given Stalin enough power to launch such adventures.

The Stalin years, 1929–1953

Notes

1 I. V. Stalin, 'Rech' na predvybornom sobranii' ['Speech at a pre-election meeting'], *Sochineniia* (Stanford, 1967), vol. 3[16], p. 6.

2 The fullest recent Russian work on this subject, based on archival sources, rejects the idea of moderate and hard-line factions in the leadership in the early 1930s: O. V. Khlevniuk, *Politbiuro: Mekahnizmy politicheskoi vlasti v 1930-e gody* [*The Politburo: Mechanisms of Political Power in the 1930s*] (Moscow, 1996), pp. 257f.

3 This point is made in two important recent articles, both based on new archival sources: Iu. N. Zhukov, 'Bor'ba za vlast' v rukovodstve SSSR v 1945–1952 godakh' ['The Struggle for Power in the Leadership of the USSR in 1945–1952'], *Voprosy istorii*, 1995, no. 1, 23–39, and Y. Gorlizki, 'Party revivalism and the death of Stalin', *Slavic Review*, 54:1 (1995) 1–22. A similar argument was made, without archival support, about the 'party revival' under Zhdanov in the late 1940s by both McCagg and Ra'anan: W. McCagg, *Stalin Embattled, 1943–1948* (Detroit, 1978) and G. Ra'anan, *International Policy Formation in the USSR* (Hamden CN, 1984). This view of Zhdanov as real challenger is rejected by the most recent Russian work: V. Zubok and C. Pleshakov, *Inside the Kremlin's Cold War* (Cambridge MA, 1996).

2

'Catch up and overtake': Stalinism and the economy

'Catch up and overtake' (*dognat' i peregnat'*) was a central slogan of the Stalin years. In one sense the Soviet history in this period *was* the history of industrialisation. As with its politics, the history of Stalinist economy also falls into distinct periods. The first ran from 1928 to 1941, and takes in the 'heroic' first three Five-year plans (1928–32, 1933–37, 1937–); the second is the period of the war; the third covers the post-war period of reconstruction, the 4th and 5th Five-year plans (1946–50, 1951–55).

Industry

The remarkable achievements of the pre-war period are one of the best-known features of the Stalin years (see Table 2.1). An industrial base was created in the first two Five-year plans: increased construction and production coincided with the geographical spread of industry into Siberia and Central Asia. The second period was the 'payoff', as the industrial base created in the 1930s was used to out-produce Nazi Germany in key areas. In the post-war period industry resumed the upward curve of production, while making good the devastation in the German-occupied regions and overcoming wartime dislocation. The history of Soviet industry across the whole of the Stalin years can be tackled through four linked questions What was achieved? Why was it achieved. How was this achievement possible? What were the implications?

*****

What was achieved? Soviet propagandists and outside observers might have come to different conclusions about the political system, but there was more agreement about the fact of the achievement in building up industry, especially in the pre-war years. In November 1929, on the twelfth anniversary of the revolution, Stalin made a speech about a 'great breakthrough' (*velikii perelom*) in industry and in agriculture. Soviet Russia had now passed, he argued, from the retreat of the NEP into a successful offensive; it had created the preconditions 'for transforming our country into a country of *metal*' (see document 4). In his 1946 election speech Stalin essentially boasted that the offensive which followed the breakthrough had achieved its objectives. '[T]o convert our country from an agrarian into an industrial one took only about thirteen years [i.e. 1928–41],' he boasted. 'One cannot help admitting that thirteen years is an unbelievably short time for accomplishing such a grandiose task.'[1] He cited 1913 and 1940, the last peace-time years before two wars: from 4.2 millions tons of steel produced in 1913 to 18.3 million in 1940; from 29 millions tons of coal to 166 million (see Table 2.1). An objective account would bring out some limitations without contradicting the basic achievement, however. The Soviet advance was not comprehensive, even within industry, and was limited to certain sectors. Quantity was achieved at the expense of quality. Reported Soviet aggregate output figures were too high, not least by failing to take account of the rising prices.

As to the wartime achievements, Stalin's 1946 boasts that Soviet rule had provided the 'material possibilities' required to beat Nazi Germany were largely true. Factories were evacuated to the east in the aftermath of Barbarossa; the scale of the evacuation – an eighth of pre-war industrial capacity – would have been impossible in an economy that was less centrally directed. Soviet industry produced 100 thousand tanks, 130 thousand aircraft, 800 thousand artillery pieces and mortars, and 30 million small arms. In the pivotal year 1943 it produced 24 thousand tanks compared with 17 thousand for Germany, 130 thousand artillery pieces compared with 27 thousand, and 35 thousand combat aircraft compared with 25 thousand. Much of this equipment was of Soviet design and in the later years of the war technically comparable to, or better than, German equivalents. There are caveats here too, however. Evacuation of industry in 1941–42 was no more a 'success' for the Russian industry than Dunkirk was for the British army – and involved great waste. The 'material possibilities' did not just come from Russia, although it is true that 'Lend-lease' aid from the US, Britain and Canada did not began to reach the USSR in quantity until 1943. Lend-lease was important in the long run for the supply of support equipment, foodstuffs, critical raw materials and even certain kinds of weapons. Most striking was the foreign supply of motor vehicles, essential for the counter-offensive of 1943–45; some 410 thousand units supplied by the Allies compared with Soviet domestic wartime production of 265 thousand. But the USSR's survival in 1941–42 was based on factors other than industrial production. The terrible human losses in the early part of the war were partly the results of the low quality of Soviet equipment, which in turn resulted from a premature military build up and from the terror of the 1937.38 purges. Soviet rule provided the 'material possibilities' required to beat Nazi Germany, but only at the cost of over ten million soldiers' lives.

Table 2.1   *Russian industrial growth under Stalin*

	1913	1927/8	1937	1940	1945	1950	1955
Cast iron (mill. t.)	4.2	3.3	14.5	14.9	8.8	19.2	33.3
Steel (mill. t.)	4.3	4.0	17.7	18.3	12.3	27.3	45.3
Coal (mill. t.)	29.0	35.4	128.0	165.9	149.3	261.1	389.9
Oil (mill. t.)	10.3	11.7	28.5	31.1	19.4	37.9	70.8
Electricity (mill. kWhs)	1.9	5.1	36.2	48.3	43.3	91.2	170.2
Motor vehicles (thou.)	–	0.8	199.9	145.4	74.7	362.9	445.3
Cotton fabrics (mill. m.)	2,582	–	3,448	3,900	1,617	3,899	5,905
Tanks	–	170	1,559	2,794	–	–	–
Combat aircraft	–	204	3,432	8,232	–	–	–

Note: A. Nove, *An Economic History of the USSR, 1971–1991* (London, 1992), pp. 4, 89, 145, 194, 228, 298, 349. Motor vehicles from *Avtomobili Rossii i SSSR*, vol. 1, Moscow, 1993, pp. 74, 160, 174, 252. Tanks and combat aircraft from R. W. Davies *et al.* (eds), *The Economic Transformation of the Soviet Union, 1913–1945* (Cambridge, 1994) , p. 298.

Stalin's 1946 speech also called for 'a new powerful upsurge of the economy', and the post-war achievement was indeed considerable. After three more Five-year plans (i.e. in 1946–60) it was intended that Russia would achieve annual production of 60 mil-

lion tons of steel and 500 millions tons of coal (see document 15).
These grandiose targets would nearly be reached by the start of
the 1958 Seven-year plan, and in some ways the industrial res-
urrection was as remarkable as what happened in the 1930s, or
in contemporary West Germany. Stalinist Russia also embarked
on a massive peace-time armament programme to complement
the Red army with a modern jet air force and a great ocean-going
navy (the former was ultimately more successful than the latter).
The most striking achievement was a vast new nuclear weapons
industry: an atomic device was tested in 1949; research work ini-
tiated under Stalin led to a thermonuclear bomb in August 1953.

*****

Why did the leaders of Soviet Russia decide on industrialisation,
and of a particular kind, rapid and with a stress on heavy industry and armaments production? Was the policy necessitated and
justified by a far-sighted vision of the need to defeat Hitler? This
achievement was the essence of Stalin's 1946 election claims, but
it also went back to his most famous speech, made fifteen years
earlier, to a conference of economic managers. It was February
1931, the height of the enthusiasm for the Five-year plan, and
Stalin suddenly introduced Russian patriotism. 'To reduce the
tempo,' argued Stalin, 'means to fall behind. Those who fall
behind get beaten. […] We are fifty to a hundred years behind
the advanced countries. We must make up this distance in ten
years. Either we do it, or we shall go under.' (see document 6).
Ten years later came the German onslaught. But such a reading
of the 1931 speech, and indeed of the late 1920s industrialisation
policy, would be misleading. In 1931, and in 1925–29 when the
industrialisation campaign was conceived and accelerated into
super-industrialisation, Germany was no danger to Russia.
Hitler was a fringe politician. Germany had been restricted by
Versailles to an army of 100,000 men, without tanks or aircraft.
Indeed, when Stalin made his 1931 speech, German soldiers
were training with forbidden equipment at secret Russian bases.
  On the other hand, preparation for war was a much more
important consideration in motivating Stalinist industrialisation
than it has been for other 'developing' countries. Industrialisation came partly from the Russian Communists' mistrust of the
outside world as much as from the existence of real enemies.

This mistrust, in turn, had roots both in the Russian tradition and in the Communists' perception of the outside world. At least since Peter the Great, Russia's rulers had promoted industry in order to fight wars and to assure the country's great power status; they had always been unusual in combining a consciousness of 'backwardness' with strong internal powers. The Communists, for their part, added an ideology of 'capitalist encirclement' and real memories of invasion by European powers and Japan in 1914–22. The regime continually emphasised what Stalin called, at either end of his career, the 'two camps', the irreconcilable conflict of capitalism and socialism (see Chapter 6). In the summer of 1927 there was a war scare, involving 'Anglo-French' imperialism, Poland and Romania to the west, and Japan to the East. It was not just Stalin who took this threat seriosly, and it did have an important influence on the decision to industrialise. But only Romania would ever attack Soviet Russia, and Britain and Poland were Stalin's allies from 1941. The post-war experience was not dissimilar although, after the experience of the 1941 surprise attack and the terrible losses suffered, a high state of preparedness was understandable. Stalin spoke in February 1946 about preparing for 'accidents' and embarked on another round of investment and belt-tightening to compete with the United States. But by that time Germany and Japan had been knocked out as major powers, and America was disarming and withdrawing from Europe; if anything Soviet policy would lead to American rearmament and redeployment. Of course, Stalinist Russia did face at certain periods real external threats, but these led to a *continuation* of a industrial and military build up that had already begun.

Like military needs, ideology was also a more important motivation for Soviet industrialisation than it was for many other 'developing' countries, and this partly explains the pace. In addition to the ideologically based conflict with the capitalist world, industrialisation was seen as an essential condition of achieving socialism (in Russia and elsewhere). The 'catch up and overtake' slogan was conceived not by Stalin in the late 1920s, but came from something that Lenin wrote in September 1917, *before* the revolution, and one of Lenin's final writings stressed the need for the new Russian state to develop the preconditions of socialism from above. Furthermore, the Communists were the party of the industrial proletariat. Employees in industry, building and transport may, according to the 1926 census, have numbered only 6 million people out of 76 million who were gainfully employed, but they were the party's constituents.

A related cause of rapid industrialisation was the character of the decision-makers. The 'great breakthrough' was the policy not just of Stalin, or a tiny group around him, but of the majority of the Communist leadership. This was the case, moreover, across two generations of the leadership. The term 'New Bolshevik' has been coined to define an influential generation of over-enthusiastic Soviet leaders who pushed through rapid industrialisation in the late 1920s and early 1930s. The group certainly existed, although this term, embracing as it does a distinction from the Old Bolsheviks, is misleading: most were veterans of the underground.[2] The term 'Stalinist' (*Stalinets*) might just as well be used. It was a revolutionary generation, young men prepared to strike out into the unknown. The civil war had been a formative experience, polarising politics, making state-military power a key instrumen, and habituating them to military means of administration. It did not matter that so many of the original revolutionary industrialisers perished in the purges of 1937–38. The successor generation of late Stalinists, sometimes called the *vydvizhentsy* (upwardly-mobile people), the 'men of '38', or the 'Brezhnev generation', were even more committed to industrialisation. They had been educated in the 1st Five-year plan period and their approach and values were reinforced by the experience of 1941–45. It was not, as Cold War historians argued, that the leaders needed an economic race to justify repression; they believed in the cause of economic modernisation.

*****

The elite wanted rapid industrialisation, but how was that industrialisation possible? How could Stalin's Russia achieve what other developing countries could not? Not all the credit lies with the system. It may seem an obvious point, but high levels of production and growth were achieved because Russia was an enormous country with rich natural resources. It also was not an economic blank slate. The new masters inherited much of value from Tsarist Russia, pre-1917 plants, a railway system and trained technicians. In addition, industrialisation, especially the initial 'take-off', owed much more than was publicly admitted to outside technology. The flagship Dnepr dam was built around American General Electric turbine-generators and constructed under American supervision. What became the Gor'kii Automobile Factory and the Stalingrad Tractor Factory were built to plans bought from Britain and America and their construction was supervised by western engineers. Many key early products of Stalinist industry were (outdated) Western designs – the Krasnyi Putilovets tractor was a Fordson, the ubiquitous GAZ-AA truck a licensed copy of the Ford AA. Later on, after 1945, recovery was assisted by the dismantling of plants in defeated Germany and by access to German technology. Reparations in the form of forced labour (POWs), plants, and raw materials came from other defeated enemies, Romania, Hungary, Finland and Japanese Manchuria. The early military build up also owed much to foreign research and development, for example, the two tanks built in largest numbers in the 1930s were license-built – but improved – copies of western designs. After the war license-built Rolls-Royce jet engines powered the first generation of jets and the Tu-4 strategic bomber was a direct copy of the American B-29 Hiroshima-bomber. We now know that espionage enabled the Russians to make a direct copy of the American plutonium bomb dropped on Nagasaki; this was the weapon tested in 1949 and code-named 'Joe-1' by US intelligence. What *was* impressive was the ability to select and acquire good designs, and the ability to develop them.

The wartime experience is a special case. How was Soviet Russia able to out-produce Nazi Germany? Some of the causes are relative and lie with shortcomings of the German war economy. It is also the case that priority had long been given in Russia to military production. The conscious development in the 1930s of resources of coal and steel, along with new engineering plants, in the Urals, western Siberia, and Central Asia would prove invaluable after the loss of the Ukraine and other parts of the western USSR in 1941–42. The level of Stalinist forethought should not, however, be exaggerated. Eastern development had other causes; only the most pessimistic planning could have assumed that so much territory would be lost. Many major industrial plants were in central and eastern European Russia (west of the Urals), in places the Germans never reached.

Leningrad was the greatest industrial centre neutralised in 'Russia'. The real losses were the the industrial towns and fuel resources of the Ukraine.

Without doubt, however, other reasons for the industrial success were 'systemic'. Most important was a very powerful state and a weak society. The system of economic administration – the party leadership, the State Planning Committee (*Gosplan*), the ministerial system, the commissariat of heavy industry (*Narkomtiazhprom*) and later the so-called branch ministries, the supervisory role of the party Central Committee – proved effective. To call the Soviet economic system 'planning' in a sophisticated economic sense is misleading, certainly in the initial period. It did not make for balanced growth of industry, or of investment versus consumption. What the system did provide was a means of rigid prioritisation, concentrating resources – especially physical resources – in key areas. An extreme example of this in peacetime was Beria's atomic bomb project. The command economy was shifted relatively easily to war production after 1941. On the other hand this should not be exaggerated. The state never had absolute control over the industrial economy and perhaps really only attempted it in 1929–32, out of naivety, and in 1941–42, out of desperation. Western students of the planning process have also stressed the importance of unofficial horizontal links between enterprises which allowed the vertical 'command-administrative' system to work.[3] Money remained part of the system and labour was relatively fluid. The fact that the system and its administrators became more sophisticated over time should not be lost sight of. The 1945–53 decade had special features which made it more than just a continuation of the 1930s; the steel of the industrial managers, the products of the cultural revolution (see p. 47) and the purges, had been tempered by the war, and they were now more experienced and trusted.

The Stalinist political regime was a necessary component of the economic success. An elaborate propaganda machine, coupled with upward mobility and popular nationalism at critical periods, won some popular support for the programme of industrialisation. The need for the extraordinary 'tempo' has been questioned; it is possible to make the case that different and more rational policies could have reached the same economic goals sooner.[4] However, it took a particular kind of motivation to set out on the road in the first place, and that motivation would be a feature of the officials who continued the policy. The darker side of the system was that the real sacrifices required by the pace and the priorities could only be achieved where workers' movements had been crushed or co-opted. Worst of all, the use of convict labour was a special characteristic of the Stalinist economic system, and its widespread use was one of the major contrasts with what came after Stalin.

*****

What were the implications? The Stalinist industrial spurt had negative as well as positive consequences. Some were visible under Stalin and others emerged later, with the extreme consequence being the economic collapse of the USSR in the 1980s. There were three inter-related elements: the nature of the command-administrative system, the priorities in the industrial economy, and the particular demands of the military-industrial complex. There is an extensive literature about the shortcomings of the administration of the Stalinist command economy, some of it coming from within Soviet Russia itself during the Khrushchev and Gorbachev periods. The 'planning' system set targets emphasising quantity at the expense of quality, and the particular rewards and punishments distorted output reports, and encouraged 'storming' (last-minute attempts to achieve targets) and hoarding – waste – of raw materials. The system was responsive to a small number of 'customers' but could not easily respond to changing demands. Technical innovation, outside narrow prioritised fields, proved difficult. The inherent inflexibility of the system was reinforced in the late 1940s and early 1950s by the elderly Stalin's non-intervention but even more by a sense that the system had proved itself in the war. The urban economy was generally distorted by its stress on heavy industry at the expense of consumer-oriented production, and investment at the expense of consumption. That there was excessive pressure on the consumer was made clear by the lowering of retail prices in April 1953 immediately after Stalin's death, the so-called 'New Course'.

Eight years after Stalin's death President Eisenhower warned Americans against the potentially 'misplaced power' of their own 'military-industrial complex'; his warning could have

applied even more to the USSR. The high share of military production was both a strength and a weakness and had short-term
and long-term consequences. This developed further after the
war, and not only with the archipelago of nuclear research centres. Paul Kennedy's analysis of the rise and fall of great powers
applies especially to the Soviet case: 'if […] too large a proportion of the state's resources is diverted from wealth creation and
allocated instead to military purposes, then that is likely to lead
to a weakening of national power over the longer term'.[5] In the
Soviet case the result was not a weakening but a collapse.

There was one other price to pay for the miracle of industrialisation, and that was to be, in human terms, the heaviest of all.

Collectivised agriculture and food supply

Stalinist Russia was a peasant country, and that is a central fact
of its economic history. According to the 1926 census there were
121 million rural inhabitants compared to 26 million urban ones.
Even in 1939, after the great migrations of the Five-year plan era,
two-thirds of the population still lived in the countryside.
During the NEP the rural economy had been organised around
25 million family farms. Trade between town and country was
unstable, and the regime had difficulties securing sufficient agricultural produce to feed the towns and the army and to provide
for exports. Forced procurement of grain was resorted to in the
winters of 1927–28 and 1928–29. Stalin spent three weeks in the
eastern part of the USSR in early 1928, and it was from this that
the 'Urals-Siberian method' of procurement took its name.
Comprehensive (*sploshnaia*) forced collectivisation, the merging
of family farms into collective farms (*kolkhozy*), followed in the
winter of 1929–30 as part of the Great Breakthrough. The rural
economy was thrown into confusion in 1930–33, culminating in
the famine of mid-1933. The new rural structure eventually settled down, and by 1937 there were 243 thousand *kolkhozy* and
four thousand state farms The war, to use Stalin's metaphor, was
as important an economic 'examination' for agriculture as it was
for industry. A major reason the war effort of Tsarist Russia fell
apart in 1916–17 was mismanagement of food supply.
Potentially the supply problem was much worse in 1941–45; the
best food-surplus areas, the Ukraine and the north Caucasus,

were lost to the Nazis in 1941–43, and the army and cities made greater demands. After the war collectivisation was extended to newly annexed territories in the west. High procurement quotas, low prices, and tax demands weighed heavily on the country-side

The rural economy did, literally, deliver the goods. The rapid industrialisation of the 1930s, and the reconstruction of the econ-omy as a whole in the late 1940s and early 1950s went ahead. The new cities were fed, as was, in wartime, a huge army. But agri-culture was not a success like the development of heavy indus-try. Hopes for agricultural exports to help pay for machinery imports were short-lived. There was no 'green' revolution. The fragile state of agriculture was brought home by the drought of 1946–47. Agricultural production in 1953, relative to the total size of the population, was still lower than it had been forty years earlier, on the eve of the First World War.

Such is an overview of development of the rural economy under Stalin. Why were these radical agrarian policies adopted? Even more than with industrialisation, the decisions were not simply economic. Most of the peasantry was perceived in Marxist class terms as petit bourgeois. The better-off peasants, the *kulaks*, were seen as influential village leaders and open ene-mies. The NEP, restoring private trade, was a concession to an enemy. On top of that was the practical problem that adminis-trative weakness in the countryside – where the majority of the population lived – contradicted the 'dictatorship of the prole-tariat'. This political confrontation between the Bolsheviks and village society will be discussed more fully in Chapter 3.

Collectivisation of the rural economy, however, had techno-cratic as well as ideological origins. Any Russian state, Marxist or non-Marxist, dictatorial or democratic, would have been con-cerned about the post-1918 state of agriculture. The 1917–18 agrarian revolution had economically been a step backwards. For many crops small family farms were not an effective use of labour, and such farms were too small fully to benefit from mechanisation. Much production was consumed on the farm and never went to market. Throughout the 1920s there was an imbalance in the availability of manufactured goods and food. The agricultural sector had to be rationalised. Exports of grain and other foodstuffs seemed necessary in order to import new foreign machinery. The keynote was 'primitive socialist accumulation', under which accumulation of the peasants' supposed surpluses would be exploited by the state to fund industrial development. While the leadership had rejected such ideas at the height of NEP, Stalin spoke publicly in July 1928 of the need for 'tribute' (*dan'*) by the peasantry to maintain the tempo of industrialisation. Events were certainly pushed forwards by the fall in peasant marketing of grain in late 1927. It may have been that the regime burnt its boats as early as the ham-fisted beginning of industrialisation, when inflation and the lack of consumer goods meant that the peasants would not market their produce even in the fitful way of the high NEP. The regime responded with a return to the forced-requisitioning policies of 1918–21, which – in a spiral of peasant resistance and bureaucratic response – led to collectivisation.

There was, especially in the initial collectivisation decision, naivety, misperception and bungling as well as bad calculation. Collectivisation was economically and politically a leap into the dark, more so even than the crash industrialisation programme. No state had ever considered 'social engineering' on such a scale, in this case involving some 25 million rural houshold, 120 million people. Stalin and his supporters were not necessarily being insincere – just massively foolish – in their hope that the mass of the peasants would voluntarily flock into collective farms. No other government would have taken such a risk. Very little advance thought was given to the precise nature of the new collective farms or even to the definition of a *kulak*.

The earlier part of this chapter discussed how the economic success of industrialisation were achieved. Agriculture was different, partly because there was in one sense no comparable economic success to explain. But how was the government able to impose its will to the extent that it did? The most important effect of collectivisation was the extension of state power. The creation of the collective farms and the destruction of village autonomy eventually made it possibility to extract grain and other produce without effective resistance. The expulsion of hundred of thousands of *kulaks* ('dekulakisation') and the migration of many of the young and active peasants to the town also lowered village resistance. Of course some peasants benefited from the state's economic policies and supported them, and the patriotism of the war years played its part. But it is also important that the regime achieved its economic objectives by, at times, showing flexibility. By the mid-1930s the regime had allowed the collective farmers to keep their acre-sized private plots and some livestock and there was a partial legalisation of the free market. By 1937 private plots produced over a third of all vegetables and two-thirds of all meat and dairy produce. In the war the regime fell back on local initiative and a freeing of controls on the private plots, although food supply in fact faced terrible difficulties. Russia was fortunate, too, that there was an exceptionally long drought-free period between 1937 and 1945 (as it had been in the critical year 1930). Russia won the war *despite* the failings of the collective farm system.

Collectivisation did further the general economic goals of the regime. It helped to provide an abundant urban labour supply, as peasants left the difficult conditions of the countryside to seek relatively better conditions on the building sites and in the factories, some of this as forced labour. It would be inaccurate to see this migration purely in rational terms, as the government did not intend the high level of movement from village to town that occurred. Stalinist policy did not create an efficient agriculture, neither did it raise the peasants' standard of living. It was significant that in his 1946 speech Stalin mentioned the near doubling not of the harvest but of 'marketable grain' (*tovarnoe zerno*) between 1913 and 1940. Overall agricultural production *per capita* did not increase. The paradox was that it was the very ability of the party-state to enforce procurements, and to achieve its short-term objectives, that made any long-term improvement of the rural economy impossible.

*****

The economic achievement of 1928–41 was not everything that Stalin boasted about in 1946. Russia was not even converted 'from an agrarian into an industrial [country]'. Industry's share of national income was still only slightly bigger than that of agriculture, and in 1939 industry still employed only 18 per cent of the labour force compared with 52 per cent for farming. In the longer term the goal was 'to catch up and overtake', and we now know that it would never be achieved.

Economic policy reflected a very high level of state power, and this had several consequences. Grave mistakes were possible; the regime may well have stumbled into both very rapid industrialisation and forced collectivisation because of its inexperience. Ironically the economic system was well suited to war, when it came in 1941. In a sense it was a war economy in peacetime and as such required little adaptation. The war was, however, a double tragedy, not only because of the losses of people and property, but also because victory seemed to confirm the effectiveness of the system.

At the time Stalin reaped personal credit for economic successes; later on he would be assigned personal responsibility for economic failures. In reality a large part of the early Communist leadership shared his mistakes, and the expansion of the 1930s and the purges put in place a new elite that internalised these policies. They would in turn dominate the USSR until the 1980s. By that time it was becoming clear that this economic system, created by Stalin and maintained by his successors, left a flawed legacy. Khrushchev had seen many of the problems of over-centralisation and the qualitative lag, but his secret speech of 1956 had accepted the achievements. Gorbachev, in his own speech on the seventieth anniversary of the October revolution (1987), was more critical. 'People had begun to believe in the universal effectiveness of rigid centralisation, and that the methods of command were the shortest and best way of resolving any problems. … A party and government leadership system of administrative command emerged in the country and red tape gained strength … [T]he administrative-command system, which had begun to take shape in the course of industrialisation and which had received a fresh impetus during collectivisation, had had an effect on the whole socio-political life of the country. Once established in the economy, it has spread to the superstructure … holding back the progress of socialist democracy.'[6]

Notes

1 Stalin, *Sochineniia*, vol. 3[16], pp. 10–13.

2 H. Hunter and J. Szymer, *Faulty Foundations: Soviet Economic Policies, 1928–1940* (Princeton NJ, 1992). This argument is also developed in M. von Hagen, *Soldiers in the Proletarian Dictatorship: The Red Army and the Soviet Socialist State, 1917–1930* (Ithaca, 1990).

3 The concept of the 'command-administrative system'; was popu-
larised by Gorbachev. Although rejected by Moshe Lewin and queried
by R. W. Davies it is still a very useful concept.

4 The clearest presentation of this view is Hunter and Szymer,
Faulty Foundations.

5 P. Kennedy, *The Rise and Fall of the Great Powers: Economic Change
and Military Conflict from 1500 to 2000* (London, 1989), pp. xvi, 496–504,
554–7.

6 M. S. Gorbachev, *Izbrannye rechi i stat'I* [*Selected Speeches and
Articles*] vol. 5, (Moscow, 1988), pp. 399, 401.

3

Peasants, workers, intelligentsia: Stalinism and society

Chapter 2 considered economic aspects of industry and agriculture in the Stalin years. The present chapter is also about workers and peasants – and their managers – but it is concerned not with levels of output or economic success or failure, but rather with indirect consequences of economic changes. As the famous *Short Course*, inspired by Stalin, put it: 'If historical science is to be a real science, it can no longer reduce the history of social development to the actions of ... "conquerors" and "subjugators" of states, but must above all devote itself to the history of the producers of material values, the history of the labouring masses, the history of peoples.'[1] Even before access to the Russian archives became easier in the late 1980s there were new currents in the study of the Stalin years. Western historians of the 1970s and 1980s – with access to some primary material and a readiness to use Stalin-era published sources – approached history 'from below' and looked closely at the peasants and workers, and also the elites, as social entities. They stressed social changes rather than purely political (or economic) ones and produced a dynamic rather than a static view. This was maintained – with even greater access to the archives – in the 1990s. The view of Soviet Russia which has emerged has been a challenge to a simplistic totalitarian interpretation.

One way of considering in general the development of Russian society in the Stalin period is to consider whether the economic revolution was paralleled by a social one. The Stalinist concept of the 'cultural revolution' is related to a sense of radical social

Stalinism and society

change and upward mobility. On the other hand, discussion of
the Stalin period, at least of that part of it after the mid-1930s, has
taken account of what the émigré sociologist Nicholas Timasheff
called the 'Great Retreat' – as a contrast to the Great
Breakthrough.[2] Retreat for Timasheff meant both a retreat from
the principles of the 1917 revolution, and a mid-1930s retreat
from the radical policies of the 1st Five-year plan era. The idea of
a socially conservative Stalinist Russia fits in with some interpretations of the period – from the totalitarian school to the
Trotskyists – that stress control and counter-revolution.

Population

Population trends indicate just how much Russia was shaken up
socially in the Stalin years. Much of what is known about population is based on four nation-wide censuses, held in 1926, 1937,
1939 and 1959. The population in 1926 has been estimated as
148.5 million, slightly higher than that of the comparable territory in 1914 (the pre-1939 borders of the USSR) – just before the
demographic catastrophe of the First World War, the revolution
and the civil war. By January 1939 the Soviet population has
been estimated to have increased to 168.9 million. This was an
increase of 20 million since 1926, but substantially less than what
would have been expected given 'normal' birth and death rates.
The infallible Stalin had announced in February 1934 that the
population could be estimated to be 168 million, based on the
1926 census and annual reported changes. Indeed the population
shortfall was such that, in a supreme act of Stalinist double-
think, the results of the January 1937 census were suppressed
and the census administrators executed. The population losses in
this period have been the subject of intensive study. There have
been a range of estimates, but a recent one, falling between
extremes, suggests that 'excess deaths' in this period, i.e. the
number of men, women and children who died prematurely,
stood at about 10 million – 8.5 million in the period 1927–36, and
1.5 million in 1937–38.[3]

The Second World War had an even greater effect on population. Eastern Poland, the Baltic republics and parts of Romania
and Finland were annexed to the USSR in 1939–40, adding more
than 20 million people, 10 per cent of a total of 197 million in

mid-1941. Four years later this population is estimated to have dropped to 170.5 million. Estimates of war losses have varied over the years, starting at 9 million in Stalin's lifetime, but with a current estimate at 26.6 million excess deaths.[4] This is distinct from a population deficit of nearly 40 million, which takes into account the wartime drop in the birth rate. The number of deaths in the Soviet armed forces is still contentious but the majority of specialists estimate it to have been 9–10 million. One official source gives the number of soldiers and sailors who were killed or died of wounds and disease as 6.9 million, with a further 4.6 million missing or captured; no fewer than 3.3 million of those captured are believed to have died in confinement; a further 3.8 million were so badly injured or ill that they were demobilised, 2.6 million of these were permanent invalids. However, the larger share of the excess deaths, roughly 15 million people, were among the civilian population. These fall under a range of categories. About 800 thousand to a million died in one episode, the blockade of Leningrad. Some 2.5 million Soviet (or 'Soviet' Polish) Jews were victims of the Nazi holocaust, and even official NKVD figures give a figure of 600 thousand who died in the terrible wartime conditions of the labour camp system, the GULAG. Nevertheless the best estimate is that some 10 million were not directly killed by the occupiers but died prematurely of illness or malnourishment; many of these were old people and children, who evidently died on both sides of the front line. This extraordinary figure of 10 million is somewhat easier to grasp if seen side-by-side with the 8.5 million excess deaths in the confusion and famine of 1927–36.[5]

The demographic catastrophe of the Stalin years, induced by the regime's politics and the Nazi invasion, is only one aspect of the population history. Another is the changing structure of society. Between 1926 and 1939 the urban population of the USSR rose from 26 million (18 per cent of the total population) to 56 million (33 per cent). Of the 30 million increase, 18.5 million came from peasant migration to the towns, another 6 million from the re-classification of particular localities as urban. Although in 1933 the government introduced passports to restrict movement (partly as a result of the 1933 famine) the net movement to the cities continued in the mid-1930s at about 2.5 million a year. By the 1959 census, six years after Stalin's death, the urban population of the USSR had increased to 101 million, 48 per cent of the total and an increase of 75 million in just over thirty years. The war also had a particular impact on society. No fewer than 34.5 million men and women served in the Soviet army and navy in 1941–45, of which perhaps three-fifths were from the countryside, i.e. 21 million peasants. On top of this there was a great movement of the civilian population with the evacuation of factories to the Urals, Siberia and Central Asia. The role of women in industrial labour was greatly increased.

Peasants and collective-farmers

The Stalinist system, as we saw in Chapter 2, sat on top of a particular peasant society. The peasants had been freed from serfdom as late as 1861, and in most of Russia a strong role in co-ordinating the family farms was played by the peasant land commune (the *mir*). Rural society had been changed by the agrarian revolution of 1917–18. The landlords had been driven away, and those peasants who had become independent farmers in the Tsarist government's pre-war reform (Stolypin's 'wager on the strong') were drawn back into the communal village. Opinions vary on the sociology of the village, with some outsiders seeing cohesion and others tension between richer and poorer peasants. In reality the *kulaks*, the better-off peasants, were rich only in a comparative sense – a *kulak* household might have a couple of horses and cows and employ a hired labourer. While there was more tension within the villages than pro-peasant politicians and historians admitted, the class lines were not as rigid or important as the Marxist view made it. The Communists, from Lenin onwards, made much of the *kulak* as a supposed representative of the counter-revolutionary layer of the rural petit bourgeoisie (the petit bourgeoisie being, in urban class terms, the shopkeepers and artisans). As we have seen, a mistrust of village society was one of the things that pushed Stalin towards collectivisation, a policy with objectives that were as much political and social as economic.

Collectivisation, beginning in 1929, had a profound effect. The villages were, within half a decade, transformed into 250 thousand collective farms, with an average of about seventy-five households on each, and their autonomy was destroyed. The central point of the *kolkhoz* (the collective farm), as far as the regime was concerned, was to guarantee food procurement, but this affected rural society more broadly. In overall charge was now the *kolkhoz* chairman who, in the early years at least, was often an outsider. More generally the village was brought more tightly under outside control through party-state organisations of the new rural district (*raion*) and by the machine-tractor stations (MTS). The peasants became part of a larger world in another sense. Dekulakisation, food procurement pressures (in its most extreme form, famine), and the employment possibilities of the new industries prompted rapid movement from village to town.

On the other hand the *kolkhoz* system settled down in the mid-1930s, and its social impact was not unlimited. The old village usually survived physically. External controls and demands were relaxed after the experiments of the early 1930s. The most recent evidence confirms that mentally the peasants were not won over to Stalin, Stalinism or even Soviet power, and their powers of passive resistance were sufficient to ensure that the plans of the regime could not be fully implemented. The idea of totalitarian political controls or an all-powerful police state, even in the 1930s, does not fit with the realities of Russian rural administration.[6] What did take place was an enfeeblement of the village, as the most energetic and mobile men and women in the countryside were attracted away to the towns, or – to put it another way – fled the hardship of the village.

It may well be that the Great Patriotic War of 1941–45 had as great an impact as the Great Breakthrough of 1929–30. *Kolkhozy* in the west of the country were in occupied territory. During the war controls on the *kolkhozy* in Soviet-held territory were reduced. Most important, tens of millions of peasants were conscripted into the Red Army or to wartime factories; many were unable or unwilling to return, and it has been estimated that only half the *survivors* of the wartime army returned to the *kolkhozy* after 1945. The early post-war era, generally neglected by historians, was another turning point. The newly annexed territories were transformed. But, above all, it was in this period – the late 1940s rather than the 1930s – that the back of the old village was finally broken. On top of the departure of so many of the young people to the towns and to the war there was the post-war merging of the *kolkhozy*, which raised the size of the organisation and meant that the *kolkhoz* was no longer based around the traditional village.

The place of the countryside in the Great Breakthrough/Great Retreat argument is peculiar. The Stalin years, including the late 1940s and early 1950s, transformed the village, and much of this was the intentional policy of the regime. Collectivisation has been described as a 'second serfdom', and indeed was seen as such by some peasants. The collective farm had more in common with the gentry estate of the years before 1917, or even before the 1861 emancipation, than the family farm of the peasant golden age 1917–30. But although the term 'second serfdom' may characterise an aspect of social relations in the countryside it misses the larger point. Serfdom had tied peasants to the land and had assumed a static society – quite the opposite of what was happening in the Stalin years.

The urban working class

Much of the controversy about the nature of Stalinist society is related to the development of the urban working class. Proponents of a Great Retreat stress the passing of the egalitarian principles of the 1917 revolution and, in the later 1930s, a move away from the worker-centred enthusiasm of the 1st Five-year plan. On the other hand other historians make much of what Stalin called the 'cultural revolution'. 'We all say that a cultural revolution is needed in our country,' he wrote in 1929. 'If we mean this seriously … we must make primary education, and later secondary education, compulsory to all citizens of the country, irrespective of their nationality … [W]ithout this there will be neither any real progress in our industry and agriculture, nor any reliable defence of our country.'[7] This educational revolution was aimed especially at the growing working class.

The urban population, as we have seen, grew very rapidly. The population of the city of Moscow grew from 2.0 million to 4.1 million between 1926 and 1939; completely new cities such as Magnitogorsk, Karaganda, Komsomolsk-na-Amure and Stalinogorsk appeared; and during the war there was a huge expansion of Urals cities such as Sverdlovsk and Cheliabinsk. Much has now been written about the Stalinist working class, especially in the heroic 1930s. The numbers of people engaged in industry, construction and transport increased from 6.3 million in 1926 to 23.6 million in 1939 and 36.6 million in 1959. There was a simultaneous movement into and out of the working class. The number of workers rose dramatically in the 1930s, but at the same time the small working class of the 1920s, and many later recruits, served as a pool for the creation of a new intelligentsia. The war brought a second transformation, as workers were conscripted in the army and their place taken by new wartime workers, many of them young women.

One aspect of state policy towards the working class was a turn from egalitarianism to stratification. Different, but related, processes were at work. The government was becoming less tolerant, even of this favoured class. The early stages of industrialisation, with the rapid growth of the work force created particular problems. There was the special problem of socialising – to use the term in a sociological rather than a political sense – the undisciplined new peasant arrivals. This policy came from the very top, and included Stalin's famous June 1931 speech calling for, among other things, wage differentials to motivate workers, and pay based on work performance (piece work). Moral incentives and, to a lesser extent, material incentives were combined in 'socialist competition', notably the 'shock work brigades' (note the military metaphor) of the 1st Five-year plan, and the Stakhanovite movement of the second. Alongside the carrot was developed the stick of labour discipline, involving notionally severe punishments for absenteeism and indiscipline, and the appearance of Soviet-trained managers who were trusted by the government to control the workplace in a way that their predecessors trained in the Tsarist era had not. Overall the Stalinist working class had to endure very difficult conditions.

Not everyone has seen this urbanisation as an advance. The historian Moshe Lewin has made much of 'ruralisation' of the cities in the 1930s as peasants flooded into them. Indeed, for him the term 'cultural revolution' is inappropriate, as in cultural terms urban Russia took a step back, only really moving forward in the 1950s.[8] While not idealising what happening in the 1930s and 1940s, however, a more balanced view would be that there was a very significant change. One aspect of this was the creation of a new intelligentsia.

The intelligentsia

In the Soviet era the Russian word *intelligentsiia* referred both to people who had received a specialist education and those who filled managerial posts. It has many shortcomings as a precise social category, and the word also conveys to English-speakers a misleading sense of intellectuality. Nevertheless it is used here as a convenient peg on which to hang a broad range of non-manual social groupings outside the peasantry and the working class. Other terms – middle class, white-collar workers, professionals, educated society, specialists, the bourgeoisie – are no more satisfactory in a Soviet context, being either inappropriate or too vague. Some other terms often applied to Communist societies – the bureaucracy, the new class, the *nomenklatura* – are also not specific enough.

The Tsarist Russia's intelligentsia – to use the term in the Soviet sense – had been divided by the events of 1917-21. Some had wholeheartedly welcomed the Bolshevik revolution and even, like Lenin, stood at its head, although these genuine enthusiasts of revolution were probably outnumbered by those who fled abroad during the Civil War. The remaining members of the intelligentsia, probably the overall majority, were neutral and lived on in the new Russia after the end of the Civil War, filling white-collar posts in government, management and education. In the early stages the system had out of necessity to rely on such 'specialists' to be industrial managers, professors, army commanders, and so on. The Great Breakthrough was accompanied by fluctuating policies of attack on, and defence of, the old intelligentsia. By June 1931 Stalin himself was explicitly requesting that support be given to 'the engineers and teachers of the "old" school', that they be protected. The survival of elements of the old intelligentsia was, however, less important than the creation of a new Soviet one. In the 1st Five-year plan era there was a conscious attempt to create a new intelligentsia from working-class and peasant recruits, using various radical forms of adult education and self-conscious promotion of workers and peasants. The best known of the last was the 'workers faculty' or *rabfak* attached to individual plants. Sheila Fitzpatrick used one Stalinist term, 'cultural revolution', to describe the process, and another, *vydvizhentsy* (roughly, the 'upwardly mobile ones'), to

49

describe the products of that revolution. An especially important strand of the new intelligentsia were the engineers.

The rise of the Stalinist intelligentsia was a not a simple revolving door, as Tsarist-era trained experts, or even a poorly trained revolutionary generation, were replaced by Soviet-trained, Red and expert, *intelligenty*. Promotion from the masses would have happened even if the regime had not believed in it for ideological reasons: the Stalinist Great Breakthrough began the creation of a vast range of new jobs in the administration of the state, the economy, and the social services. The terror of 1937–38, dealt with more fully in Chapter 7, was not necessarily linked to upward movement, as many *vydvizhentsy* were killed. Nevertheless, those who died in 1937-1938 were replaced by the younger generation who had been educated in the Soviet era. It is possible that Stalin saw the mass purge primarily as a means of getting rid of poorly educated or impractical revolutionaries and replacing them with a new generation with technical training, but it is more likely that this was only secondary factor. Once – for other reasons – it had been decided that a large number of people had to be purged, it was helpful that they were not considered to be irreplaceable.

Both positive and negative consequences stemmed from the new intelligentsia. Insofar as the economic revolution was a success, and the Soviet system was stable, the new intelligentsia contributed to it. From the regime's point of view the cultural revolution provided a politically reliable intelligentsia. On the other hand this group was not well educated, and were narrowly specialised; as in other areas of Stalinist life corners were cut and the work of creation was left unfinished. The bulk of new managerial posts in the 1930s and 1940s were held by promoted shop floor workers without formal theoretical training, the so called *praktiki*. More broadly it has been argued by Moshe Lewin and others that this new elite was psychologically akin to the peasantry or the urban lower middle class. Part of Lewin's influential general argument about the Stalinist experience – which owes a great deal to both the Mensheviks and to Trotsky – is that system was contaminated by the very mass of rural Russia that it was trying to overwhelm, and that this was especially true in the new administrative layers, who were transformed by *muzhik* (peasant) values. Nevertheless, as with the urban working class, the creation of a new intellgentsia, no matter how imperfect, was not, on balance, a retreat. And, however one sees the new intelligentsia, it had a long impact on the history of the country. Forged under Stalin in the 1930s, it would be the dominant force through the 1960s and 1970s.

******

Other aspects of social policy can be touched upon here only briefly and where they are relevant to the Great Retreat debate. As elsewhere there were contradictory trends. There was the strengthening of the conventional family from the mid-1930s, yet women played an important part in this new urban work force. More and more women were employed outside the home, from 29 per cent in 1928 to 40 per cent in 1940, yet women tended to be concentrated in lower-paid jobs, a situation that would continue after Stalin's death. There was a stress on traditional education rather than the 'progressive methods' of the 1920s, but this was part of a great expansion of the educational system (see document 16B). There was a greater tolerance for the Russian Orthodox Church, especially under the wartime revival of Russian nationalism. In the suppressed January 1937 census a remarkable number of people declared themselves religious believers: of 98 million individuals aged over fifteen years, 42 million declared themselves to be Orthodox Christians and 8 million to be Muslims; some 42 million declared themselves non-believers – 43 per cent of the total, although this element was stronger among literate and younger people (57 per cent of those aged 16–29).[9] The regime's policy toward culture and the creative intelligentsia was also relevant; this will be discussed more fully in Chapter 4.

The social historians have provided a corrective to the simple, static and control-focused totalitarian view showing the Stalinist social reality of the 1930s and 1940s to be extremely dynamic and, to a remarkable extent, out of control. Following the Great Breakthrough, the Great Retreat only gave form to what might be called a Great Advance. The advance was, to be sure, not fully successful even in its own terms, any more than the economic revolution of the Great Breakthrough was complete. Overall the picture throughout this period is one of a society in upheaval, what Moshe Lewin has called a 'quicksand society'.[10] This upheaval was not just the result of the social engineering of the Stalinist Great Breakthrough, however; other causes were the long-term consequences of the 1917 revolution and the German invasion. When Stalin died the majority of the population still lived in the countryside, and although there were winners as well as losers, and the former provided the cement of Stalinism, the regime did not achieve its aims of winning over or subduing the population. This was no Orwellian super-state, although the main social groups were themselves in such a state of flux that they could pose no effective alternative of their own. Nevertheless the regime could not overcome the resistance of the mass of the population, and it had to accept limitations and compromises.

A more solid society eventually coalesced at the end of the Stalin years, making them a crucial period in Russian history. Looking at the twenty-five years of Stalin's power there are strong, and clear currents: the migration from the villages to towns (with consequences for both), the enlargement and stratification of the urban working class, the creation of the new Soviet intelligentsia. All of this might have happened anyway as a result of the 1917 revolution, or from natural generational change, but it would have happened more slowly. This social revolution had as profound an effect as the parallel economic modernisation or the evolution of the political dictatorship. Indeed, the changes in society in the Stalin years in the long term undermined the system. An urbanised, literate society, with a large educated sector, could not in the end be run along Stalinist lines; this had become clear by the 1980s. The Stalinist regime had indeed attempted to mobilise society for its own purposes, but it was impossible for the 'mobilisation state' to implant just those features of modernity that were useful to it.

Notes

1   *History of the Communist Party of the Soviet Union (Bolsheviks): Short Course* (Moscow, 1939), p. 121.

2   Nicholas Timasheff, *The Great Retreat: The Growth and Decline of Communism in Russia* (New York, 1946). Timasheff's ideas were effectively used as an analytical tool in Sheila Fitzpatrick's *The Russian Revolution* (Oxford, 1994).

3   S. Wheatcroft and R. W. Davies, 'Population', in R.W. Davies *et al.*
(eds), *Economic Transformation in the Soviet Union* (Cambridge, 1994), p.
77. This, along with other articles in this book, is a basic source for the
present chapter. There is now a translation of the preliminary findings
of the 1937 census: Iu. A. Poliakov, 'A half century of silence', *Russian
Studies in History*, 31:1 (1992), pp. 1–98.

4   M. Ellmann, and S. Maksudov, 'Soviet deaths in the Great Patriotic
War', *Europe-Asia Studies*, 46:4 (1993), pp. 671–80. Other information in
this section comes from G. F. Krivosheev (ed.), *Soviet Casualties and
Combat Losses in the Twentieth Century* (London, 1997).

5   Wheatcroft and Davies, *Economic Transformation*, pp. 77, 79.
Another version, a preliminary but plausible breakdown by leading
demographers of 17 million civilian deaths, suggested 7 million excess
deaths in Leningrad and the German-occupied areas, including 3 million Jews. As many as 7 million were the result of the worsening living
conditions in the Soviet-controlled areas, and in addition 3 million died
in the camps or among deported ethnic minorities; a further 2 million
emigrated, mainly to Poland (Ellman and Maksudov, 'Soviet deaths',
p. 680n21). This is in contrast even to late glasnost era estimates, in
which all excess civilian deaths were in German-held territory.

6   Two recent books on this important subject, based on archival
research, are S. Fitzpatrick, *Stalin's Peasants: Resistance and Survival in the
Russian Village after Collectivization* (Oxford, 1995), and L. Viola, *Peasant
Rebels under Stalin: Collectivization and the Culture of Peasant Resistance*
(New York, 1996).

7   I. V. Stalin, 'National'nyi vopros i leninizm' ['The national question and Leninsim'], *Sochineniia*, vol. 11, p. 354.

8   M. Lewin, *The Making of the Soviet System: Essays in the History of
Interwar Russia* (London, 1985), pp. 38, 41.

9   Poliakov, 'A half century', pp. 66–8.

10   Lewin, *Making*, p. 44.

4

Socialist realism:
Stalinism and culture

In terms of Russian cultural history, the 1920s have been more attractive to western intellectuals than the 1930s and 1940s. A cultural avant-garde flourished in the NEP decade, and innovative work in cinema, art, architecture, literature and music have fascinated even those critical of other aspects of Communism. Ironically this avant-garde would later be rejected or ignored in Russia itself as 'formalism', and that rejection would continue until near the end of the Communist period (see document 16). The avant-garde was replaced in the 1930s, in a cultural 'retreat', by something much more conservative. This new culture would be ridiculed in the west and aspects specific to the Stalin years would, after 1953, be ignored, forgotten or hidden away even in the USSR. One of the reasons for a much greater interest in, and access to, Stalinist culture has been *glasnost*; a secondary factor has been the international rise of post-modernism, especially in the visual arts and architecture.

Imperial Russia, for all its economic and political backwardness, had developed a world culture in literature, music, dance and the theatre, and a strong national tradition in art and architecture. The post-1917 Soviet state was also interested in culture; the revolution was to a degree led by part of the intelligentsia, and the intelligentsia as a whole had traditionally had a strong radical component, but the authoritarian side of the revolutionary era should not be minimised. Among the two million who emigrated abroad after the revolution were many members of the creative intelligentsia. For its part the new regime had, well before Stalin's ascendancy, established what has been aptly described as a 'propaganda state', and in the 1920s the members of the old creative intelligentsia who had remained in Russia worked under the relatively loose overall control of Lunacharskii, head of the Commissariat of Education (*Narkompros*).[1] Another feature of Soviet Russia in the 1920s which, paradoxically, contributed to the visionary quality of its art was its poverty. Architecture, for example, was largely limited to sketches rather than ferroconcrete, while cinema was restricted by lack of film stock; even publishing was made difficult by paper shortages. A symbol of this period was the artist Tatlin's 1919 design for the 'Monument to the Third International', a combination of the Tower of Babel and a roller coaster, and intended to be twice the size of the Empire State building.

The late 1920s were characterised not so much by state domination over the creative intelligentsia (although there was censorship of various kinds) but by conflict between the majority of the old intelligentsia who were prepared to work within the regime – the 'fellow travellers' – and those of a new generation who were striving to establish 'proletarian' hegemony over culture. The late 1920s, and especially the 1st Five-year plan era, the years of the 'cultural revolution', saw a mushrooming of competing groups. The onset of rapid 'socialist construction' coincided with regime-sponsored criticism of pre-revolutionary experts; the 1928 Shakhty trial involved mining engineers trained under the old regime, but it weakened the position of the old intelligentsia as a whole. The best-known organisation on the cultural 'front' was RAPP (the Russian Association of Proletarian Writers), which fiercely attacked 'fellow travellers'.

The nature of Soviet culture and the way in which it was to be organised were resolved at about the same time. These decisions did not take place in isolation. Society was changing; economic modernisation and mass education were becoming priorities, and political control from the centre was becoming stronger. Stalin's June 1931 speech about the value of the Tsarist-educated intelligentsia signalled another change of policy. A party resolution of April 1932 laid down a general cultural policy abolishing aggressive and competing proletarian organisations. The literary intelligentsia, for example, were to have a single 'Writers Union'. The main objective was 'the mobilisation of Soviet writers and artists around the tasks of socialist construction', and cultural organisations were not to cut themselves off from 'a considerable number of writers and artists sympathetic towards socialist construction'. The personification of this new line was the novelist Maksim Gor'kii (real name A. M. Peshkov) a gritty realist writer who had gone into self-imposed exile after 1917 but who returned permanently in the early 1930s to be feted by the regime. The main street of Moscow was renamed in his honour, as was his birthplace, the big city of Nizhnii Novgorod. It took a remarkably long time to set up the system, and indeed the Writers Union was only inaugurated in April 1934. Parallel organisations were created in other cultural fields, although not in a uniform way. The Union of Composers and the Union of Architects appeared in 1932, but the Union of Artists and the Union of Cinematographers would be post-Stalin creations; the artists had revived republican Academies of Arts. Although the unions were supposed to be broadly based this was, like so much else in the Stalin period, illusory: the second congress of the Writers Union would not convene until twenty years after the first.

Although Stalin never spoke publically about art or culture he played a direct role by his personal communication with selected writers, artists, architects, and film-makers; in the case of writers this sometimes even involved seeing drafts of their work. He protected the poet Pasternak and the dramatist and satirist Bulgakov, and was a patron of the film director Eisenstein. He also intervened at a more strategic level. At a hastily-called evening meeting at Gor'kii's Moscow town house in October 1932 about fifty writers were joined by Stalin and his Politburo lieutenants Molotov, Voroshilov and Kaganovich. Apart from expressing a preference for the plays over novels and poetry (the workers – and presumably Stalin – did not have time for leisure reading), he repeated the notion of 'a strong nucleus of Communists and around them a wide strata of non-party writers'; he concluded by calling the creative intelligentsia the 'engineers of human souls' (see document 8). Stalin also crystallised at this point what would be, up to 1991, the key concept for Soviet culture: 'socialist realism'. Andrei Zhdanov, the party's cultural 'expert' for fourteen years, outlined this doctrine to the first congress of the Writers Union in April 1934. He compared the decadence of modern bourgeois culture with a Soviet alternative that would combine realism (and accessibility to the masses) with a utopian vision that happened to coincide with the party's programme (see document 9). By the time Zhdanov spoke the genre was already in practice, embodied in a collective account praising the construction of the Leningrad–White Sea (Belomor) canal, a showpiece of economic transformation and an early product of convict labour.

The clarification of policy from 1932 involved not only a greater tolerance of the old intelligentsia, it was also a response to an audience, and some historians have argued that this shows the power of that audience.[2] In literature the emphasis was on intelligibility and also a return to the classics: the wide celebration of the centenary of the poet Pushkin in 1937 (coinciding with the great terror) would be an important symbol. The changes in the area of literature were paralleled by changes, in the same spirit of socialist realism, anti-formalism and accessibility, in all areas of Soviet culture. In the 1930s, for example, Soviet film developed rapidly, moving away from artistic and technical experimentation to genuinely popular films. Painting and sculpture rejected the abstract experiments of the 1920s and turned to a representational style comprehensible to everyone and celebrating the same themes as in literature. There was a stress on team production, and art played much the same function as commercial advertising in capitalist societies, for example in its extensive use of images of the leader, a central feature of these years. This was not unique to the Stalin period, as the Lenin cult had been developed early on and would continue after 1953. Lenin himself had in 1918 put forward a 'Plan for Monumental Propaganda'. But the extent of the attention paid to a living leader, especially from the middle of the 1930s, was extraordinary.

In architecture the competition for the 'Palace of Soviets' was an important milestone. The palace was to be the most central symbol of the new system, the proposed headquarters of the Soviet government. It was to have been built just to the west of the Kremlin, on the site of the giant Cathedral of Christ the Redeemer (dynamited in December 1931 and rebuilt in the 1990s). After a number of 'international modern' designs were put forward, one by the sympathetic Swiss architect Le

Corbusier, a design was adopted in 1934 that was both enormous and architecturally conservative, a 300 metre tower (taller than the Empire State Building) and topped by a 100 metre statue of Lenin (taller than the Statue of Liberty). Stylistically the project used classical forms, which was extended throughout Soviet architecture. The fact that the palace was never finished, and was probably inherently unfinishable, was characteristic of the Stalin years and of its culture. In the decade after the Second World War five Gothic skyscrapers *were* erected to dominate the skyline of Moscow; the best known of these was the building of Moscow State University. Typically, for the post-war era, these were built in a more nationalist, Muscovite style, borrowing from the details of the Kremlin.

In early 1936 the party's policy took a more restrictive turn with party pronouncements about shortcomings in different aspects of cultural life. One of the first was criticism that January of Shostakovich's opera *Lady Macbeth of Mtsensk*, and in the following months came party decrees against 'formalism' in architecture and painting. Formalism in any art form was never clearly defined, except in a negative sense – non-accessible, non-realistic, non-socialist. The following year the cultural elite was caught up in the purges; as many as 1,500 writers perished, among them the poet Mandelshtam, the theatre director Meyerhold, the writers Babel' and Pil'niak. The cultural community were also called out to join in the collective condemnation of 'enemies of the people'.

Like so many aspects of the Stalin years there was no single unchanging cultural policy. The arts served whatever were the highest priorities of the regime, although they also reflected genuine changes in national sentiment. In the late 1930s, as Europe moved closer to a new general war, patriotism and national defence became more important themes. During the war itself this continued to be the focus; indeed culture had a lower 'ideological' content, and writers, artists and film-makers shared the objectives of the regime. The socialist patriotism of the pre-war years, extolling the exclusive superiority of the new socialist system and condemning the pernicious nature of capitalism, was replaced by a Russian patriotism, extolling the virtues both of Russian traditions and Russian socialism, between which no contradiction was seen. Once the war was over, however, there was a renewed emphasis on the particular interests of the regime, a reaffirmation of the centrality of both Stalin and the party. The retrenchment was again associated with Zhdanov and began with party decrees of August 1946 criticising the literary journals *Zvezda* and *Leningrad* (see document 16A). More emphasis was placed on the rejection of western models. This stress on Russian themes partly reflected the political paranoia of the Cold War years, and Stalin's own vanity and paranoia. In the late 1940s the cult of Stalin reached its peak, especially in the celebrations to mark the great man's (supposed) 70th birthday in 1949. Cultural terror of a sort continued, most notorious being the case of Jewish actor and playwright Mikhoels, apparently murdered by the secret police. For the most part, however, by the late 1940s cultural repression replaced physical repression, at least amongst the creative intelligentsia. Although the satirist Zoshchenko and the poetess Akhmatova were bitterly criticised by Zhdanov they survived. In addition there is a sense in which Soviet culture came in the aftermath of the war to reflect the attitudes of a key part of the population. One influential analysis has been based on a 'big deal' in this period between the regime and an emerging self-confident and materialist middle-class elite.[3]

******

The legacy of Stalinist cultural policy was ambiguous. Not much of High Stalinist art survives – although it is still difficult to ignore the 'Stalin Gothic' skyscrapers in Moscow. Nevertheless the doctrine of socialist realism and the institutions of cultural control survived Stalin's death and even Khrushchev's 'thaw'. Culture, to the end of the Communist period, was dominated by a watered-down version of the Stalinist model. The doctrine of socialist realism and the system of state-controlled culture proved as enduring as the collective farms or one-party elections.

Many aspects of Stalinist culture were not unique, either in comparison with other periods in Russian history or with other states, both totalitarian and non-totalitarian. It is indeed in this area of culture that the broad idea of totalitarianism is most convincing – despite the fact that culture was not a special feature in the best-known 'model' of totalitarianism, that of Friedrich and

Brzezinski.[4] A number of writers have pointed to the striking formal similarities between Stalinist art, the art of Nazi Germany and, to a lesser extent, that of Fascist Italy. 'In a totalitarian system art performs the function of transforming the raw material of dry ideology into the fuel of images and myths intended for general consumption. The precise nature of the raw material ... is of no more importance than whether one uses beet or wheat when distilling alcohol.'[5] 'Realistic' Stalinist art did not depict reality, it depicted utopia. Stalinist Russia, Nazi Germany and Fascist Italy shared a common concern with mass mobilisation, and they were also united in a rejection of what they regarded as contemporary 'bourgeois culture'.

It could be argued that Stalinist culture fits into the pattern of the Great Retreat. From an atmosphere of radical experimentation during the NEP, Stalinism turned back to a much more conservative approach to culture. In fact, the situation was more complicated than that. Control of culture and mass communication was something which Lenin had stressed since the beginning of Soviet rule; in addition the art of Tatlin and the work of defeated proletarian writers, artists and theorists were in a sense more 'totalitarian' or intolerant than many of those 'accessible' writers and artists who were favoured from the 1930s.[6] Again, form and content must not be confused. Stalinist culture embraced many of the traditions of the culture of nineteenth-century Tsarist Russia: realistic, accessible, didactic literature, art and music – it even embraced classicism. But the content of what was produced in this realistic way was 'modern': it was promoted to achieve objectives which the regime chose to stress – economic activity, the socialist utopia, national defence and adulation of the leader – and some of this, at least, it had in common with the avant-garde of the 1920s. Stalin's metaphor of 'engineers of human souls' was very telling. Finally, the culture of the Stalin years reflected a changing – advancing rather than retreating – society. Much of it was a product of modernisation and technology, just as was the case in other countries. The appearance of mass culture, popular fiction, cinema, radio and spectator sports in the 1920s, 1930s and 1940s went hand-in-hand with twentieth-century urbanisation. Stalinist culture was mass culture, and indeed one of the features of the period was a self-conscious breaking down of the distinction between high and low culture, a culture for an educated elite and a culture for the masses. That this was possible was symptomatic of how much society was changing.

Notes

1　P. Kenez, *The Birth of the Propaganda State: Soviet Methods of Mass Mobilization, 1917–1929* (Cambridge, 1985).

2　See, for example, the introduction to J. von Geldern and R. Stites (eds), *Mass Culture in Soviet Russia* (Bloomington IN, 1995).

3　V. Dunham, *In Stalin's Time: Middleclass Values in Soviet Fiction* (Durham, 1990). The influential Sovietologist Jerry Hough, in his preface, suggested that the 'big deal' actually dated back to the 1930s (p. xxviii).

4　C. Friedrich and Z. Brzezinski, *Totalitarian Dictatorship and Autocracy*, 2nd ed., (Cambridge MA, 1965).

5　I. Golomstock, *Totalitarian Art in the Soviet Union, the Third Reich, Fascist Italy and the People's Republic of China* (London, 1990), p. xii.

6　For differing views on the contribution of the avant-garde to 'totalitarian' socialist realism see the articles by Rakitin and Groys in H. Günther (ed.), *The Culture of the Stalin Period* (Basingstoke, 1990).

5

The unbreakable union: Stalinism and the nationalities

Stalin's 1946 election speech also raised the nationalities question. Prominent journalists had claimed that 'the Soviet multi-national state is an "artificial and unviable structure," that in the event of any complications the collapse of the Soviet Union would be inevitable, that the Soviet Union would share the fate of Austria-Hungary'. Here, as elsewhere, however, the war had shown that the system had 'passed the examination'; it was a system 'in which the national problem and the problem of co-operation among nations (*natsii*) have been solved better than in any other multi-national state'.[1]

After December 1991 and the replacement of the Soviet Union by the Commonwealth of Independent States the perspective is very different. Student riots in Kazakhstan in 1986 were followed by civil war between Armenians and Azerbaidzhanis in Nagorno-Karabakh. In 1987 mass demonstrations in the Baltic states – annexed by Stalin – and sit-ins near the Kremlin by Crimean Tatars – deported by Stalin – moved the nationalities question to the top of Gorbachev's agenda. Within four years the Gorbachev government was forced to accept the secession of the Baltic republics and a fundamental change in the relationship between the other nations. This confrontation would bring about his downfall and that of the USSR. The Soviet Union *had* shared the fate of Austria-Hungary, and this had happened without a major war.

The nationalities and the national flowering

The Russian nationalities question was not unique to Stalin's time. Stalin inherited the bulk of the pre-1914 multi-national 'Russian' empire. The nature of the nationalities 'problem' and the ability of successive Russian governments to keep the empire together cannot be understood without a sense of the basic ethnic make-up, as shown in Table 5.1 (based on the 1926, 1939 and 1959 censuses). In 1939 half the population were not Russian, 99.6 million out of 170.6 million – and this was before the annexation of another 20 million non-Russians in 1939–40. However there were more ethnic Russians (*russkie*) than any other group. The Ukrainians were a special case in terms of size, but leaving them aside no other minority was more than one-fifteenth the size of the Russians. The Russians, Ukrainians and Belorussians – together 78 per cent of the total in 1939 – all spoke similar Slavic languages and had a broadly similar cultural background. The only other nationalities over 3 million even in 1959 were the Uzbeks and Kazakhs of Central Asia. The major Transcaucasian nationalities were each under 3 million and the Baltic nations were smaller still. Another general factor is that conflict between minorities was as serious as that between Russians and minorities. It is precisely the ethnic diversity of the Soviet geographic 'space' – a hundred and more distinct nationalities – that made ethnic Russian hegemony, under the Tsars, under Brezhnev and under Stalin, possible. The Russian situation was quite different from that of Europe's other multi-national empire, Austria-Hungary. There the 'master' German nation made up only 24 per cent of the population, alongside a Hungarian minority that was almost as large (20 per cent) and two Slav groups that were 10 per cent or more, the Czechs (13 per cent) and the Poles (10 per cent).

The nationalities question was one to which Lenin and the Bolsheviks had devoted special attention, given the revolutionary potential of the nationalities within the Russian empire. Stalin's place in all this was special. Dzhugashvili-Stalin was himself a Georgian (*gruzin*), a member of one of the national minorities, born in a region that had been part of the Russian Empire for less than eighty years. He was a product of Russification, who evidently began to learn the Russian

The Stalin years, 1929–1953

Table 5.1   *Nationalities of the Stalin-period USSR (millions)*

	1926	1939	1959	
Core Slavs				
Ethnic Russians	77.8 [53%]	99.6 [58%]	114.1 [55%]	
Ukrainians	31.2	28.1	37.3	expanded 1940
Belorussians	4.8	5.3	7.9	expanded 1940
Baltic				
Lithuanians	0.0	0.0	2.3	annexed 1940
Latvians	0.1	0.1	1.4	annexed 1940
Estonians	0.2	0.1	1.0	annexed 1940
Moldavians	0.3	0.3	2.2	annexed 1940
Transcaucasus				
Georgians	1.8	2.2	2.7	
Azeri	1.7	2.3	2.9	
Armenians	1.6	2.2	2.8	
Central Asia				
Kazakhs	4.0	3.1	3.6	
Uzbeks	3.9	4.8	6.0	
Tadzhiks	1.0	1.2	1.4	
Turkmen	0.8	0.8	1.0	
Kirgiz	0.8	0.9	1.0	
Non-Republic				
Tatars	2.9	4.3	5.0	
Jews	2.6	3.0	2.3	
Mordvinians	1.3	1.5	1.3	
Germans	1.2	1.4	1.6	
Chuvash	1.1	1.4	1.5	
Poles	0.8	0.6	1.4	
Bashkirs	0.7	0.8	1.0	
Other	6.4	6.6	7.1	
Total	147.0	170.6	208.8	

Source: G. Simon, *Nationalism and Policy toward the Nationalities in the Soviet Union* (Boulder CO, 1991), pp. 372–5. Listing gives all groups with a total population of over one million in 1959. 'Non-republic' is those groups which did not have their own union republic. The 1939 figures are for January, i.e. before the annexation of the western territories. These figures are not exactly the same as some of the total population figures given earlier; these are the official figures, while some figures in Chapter 3 include demographers' correctives.

language when he entered the Gori Ecclesiastical Seminary at age eight. Stalin's first important 'theoretical' work was 'Marxism and the National Question', an essay published under Lenin's sponsorship in the spring of 1913; his first post in the Soviet government was as head of the people's commissariat for nationalities (*Narkomnats*).

The Communists' approach to the nationalities question, at least as it evolved in the later part of the civil war, was certainly more subtle and effective than that of the Tsarist government in its final decades or of their White opponents, whose slogan had been 'Russia, one and indivisible!'. There was another paradox here. The Communists had, as Marxists, made conflict between ethnic groups secondary to conflict between classes, and as Leninists they advocated a centralised party and state structure. On the other hand the pre-revolutionary Bolshevik party had attracted ethnic as well as social 'outsiders'. The central leadership under Lenin and Stalin was very different from what had gone before, or what would come afterwards. In the Communist elite (Central Committee members) in the first two decades of Soviet power, ethnic Russians made up only about 50 per cent.

The nationality-based political structure, like so much else, developed during the civil war, when nominally independent socialist states were set up. These merged in December 1922 into the 'Union of Soviet Socialist Republics' whose formal structure was laid down in the constitutions of 1924 and further developed in the 1936 'Stalin Constitution'. The federal system involved a complex hierarchy of nationality elements, 'union republics' (SSRs), 'autonomous republics' (ASSRs), 'autonomous regions' (AOs) and so on, but the USSR changed rapidly under Stalin's control in the 1930s and 1940s. Initially there were only four union republics – a Russian Socialist Federative Soviet Republic (RSFSR), the Ukrainian Soviet Socialist Republic (SSR), the Belorussian SSR and the Transcaucasian Socialist Federative Soviet Republic (ZSFSR). More union republics were created in the 1920s and 1930s, mostly in Central Asia, and in 1939 several new ones were set up in the annexed western territories. By 1940 there were sixteen union republics (see Table 5.2). Within the RSFSR there were a large number of autonomous republics, twenty-one in 1939, some of which had a population larger than that of the smaller union republics.

Table 5.2   *The union republics of the Stalin-period USSR and their ethnic composition*

	estab.	1926				1939				1959			
		p	t	r	o	p	t	r	o	p	t	r	o
Russ. SFSR	1917	101.0	73	73	27	108.3	83	83	17	117.5	83	83	17
Uk. SSR	1919	29.0	80	9	11	31.8	73	13	14	41.9	77	17	7
Bel. SSR	1919	5.0	81	8	12	5.6	83	6	11	8.1	81	8	11
Est. SSR	1940	–	–	–	–	–	–	–	–	1.2	75	20	5
Lat. SSR	1940	–	–	–	–	–	–	–	–	2.1	62	27	11
Lit. SSR	1940	–	–	–	–	–	–	–	–	2.7	79	8	12
Kar. SSR	1939	0.3	37	57	5	0.5	23	63	14	0.7	13	63	23
Mol. SSR	1940	–	–	–	–	–	–	–	–	2.9	65	10	24
Georg. SSR	1936	2.7	67	4	29	3.5	61	9	30	4.0	64	10	26
Azeri SSR	1936	2.3	62	9	28	3.2	58	16	25	3.7	67	14	19
Arm. SSR	1936	0.9	84	2	14	1.3	83	4	13	1.8	88	3	9
Kazakh SSR	1936	6.5	57	20	23	6.1	38	40	21	9.3	30	43	27
Uzbek SSR	1925	5.3	66	5	29	6.3	64	11	24	8.1	62	13	24
Kirgiz SSR	1936	1.0	67	12	22	1.5	52	21	27	2.1	40	30	29
Turk. SSR	1925	1.0	72	7	21	1.3	59	19	22	1.5	61	17	22
Tadzhik SSR	1929	0.8	75	1	25	1.5	60	9	31	2.0	53	13	34

Source: Simon, *Nationalism and Policy*, pp. 376–89. Abbreviations in the columns are the following: Russ. = Russian; Uk. = Ukrainian; Bel. = Belorussian; Est. = Estonian; Lat. = Latvian; Lit. = Lithuanian; Kar. = Karel–Finn.; Mol. = Moldavian; Georg. = Georgian; Arm. = Armenian; Turk. = Turkmen; estab. = date of establishment of union republic, p = total population (millions), t = per cent of 'titular' nationality (e.g. Ukrainians in Ukrainian SSR), r = % of ethnic Russians, o = % of others. Simon's table simplifies a very complex situation; for 1926, especially, some regions are counted twice, i.e. within the RSFSR (and other areas) and as the union republics they later became.

Moscow had a great deal of *de facto* political control from the beginning, and after some experimentation in the civil war neither the Red army nor the Communist party were organised on a federal basis. However, this territorialisation was psychologically very important for many of the ethnic groups, who until this time had had an identification only with larger supranational cultural factors (for example, Islam). It also contributed to a situation in which the cities – administrative centres – in the minority regions came to be dominated by the natives rather than outsiders. The structure was one which Lenin had forced through over Stalin's opposition; the commissar for nationalities had preferred 'autonomisation': the absorption of the three non-

Russian entities (the Ukraine, Belorussia, and Transcaucasia) within a Russian federation.

It was at the height of the NEP that Stalin formulated the concept that culture under socialism would be 'proletarian in its content, national in its form'.[2] Nationalities policy at this time centred around 'nativisation' (*korenizatsiia*, sometimes translated as 'indigenisation'). Soviet power created roots (*kornii*) within the native peoples, recruiting members of the national minorities to state and party posts within their own regions. It encouraged national cultures, developing local languages, and publishing newspapers and books in those languages. The idea of the 'flowering' (*rastsvet*), was also broadly used in the 1920s and early 1930s by Stalin and others. Although the term *korenizatsiia* was not widely used after the 1920s, the policy was never abandoned. The regime favoured it in the 1920s as a means of broadening its political base, and by the end of the decade it was needed for other reasons, as Stalin made clear in a March 1929 article: the 'cultural revolution' required making 'primary education and later secondary education compulsory for all citizens of the country, irrespective of their nationality. Why [schools, and administrative apparatus, and cultural institutions working] in the native languages? – it may be asked. Because only in their native, national languages can the vast masses of the people be successful in cultural, political and economic development.'[3]

The Great Breakthrough and the nationalities

The direct and indirect economic consequences of industrialisation and collectivisation (especially the famine of early 1933) were especially felt in certain national regions. The peasants of the Ukrainian SSR suffered heavily, as did the nomads of the Kazakh ASSR. The most complete Western study of Stalinist nationalities policy concludes that the Stalin regime was sincere about the value of nativisation, but executed an about-turn in favour of the ethnic Russians and of centralisation when the 'revolution from above' met resistance in the early 1930s.[4] This is probably an oversimplification, but the evident change in nationalities policy did follow 'logically' from the development of a centrally planned economy.

The process of industrialisation in the minority areas was mixed. Two flagship projects of the early period were built in non-Russian areas – the Dnepr hydroelectric dam in the Ukraine and the 1,500 kilometre Turksib railway, linking Central Asia and Siberia; there was a substantial movement of ethnic Russians and Ukrainians into Central Asia. On the other hand most of the pre-war heavy industrial development was either in the Russian federation (post-1936 borders) or the Ukrainian SSR, although the wartime industrial spurt did lead to some relocation of plants into Central Asia as well as Siberia. The urbanisation which had such a massive impact on Soviet society in general – an increase from 18 per cent urbanised in 1926 to 33 per cent in 1939 and 48 per cent in 1959 – naturally also affected the nationalities. The ethnic Russians stayed ahead of the other pre-1940 nationalities, with 21 per cent, 38 per cent and 58 per cent urbanised. The rise, however, was also spectacular among the minority nationalities. Urbanised Ukrainians shot up from 10 per cent in 1926 to 29 per cent in 1939, with a further rise to 39 per cent in 1959, and the comparable figures for the Belorussians was 10 per cent, 21 per cent and 32 per cent. The Central Asian peoples lagged behind. Uzbeks and Kazakhs were, respectively, only 15 per cent and 16 per cent urban in 1939, although their urbanised proportions had increased to 22 and 24 per cent by 1959.[5] Urbanisation also affected ethnic nationalism, as for the first time the towns were predominantly of the same nationality as the surrounding hinterland. Before the 1920s the towns had been dominated, depending on the area, by ethnic Russians, Jews, Poles and Armenians. The process of Russification of urban migrants which had taken place under the old regime now ceased, however the process of modernisation also led to a substantial migration of Russians into the other republics. Table 5.2 illustrates this: the Kazakh SSR (ASSR to 1936) was a special case as Russians rose from 20 per cent to 40 per cent there between 1926 and 1939, although big increases can be seen in nearly every republic.

Once the 'socialist offensive' was under way it was clearer than ever that the creation of an all-union economy (and state) ran counter to any further nationality-based fragmentation. Russian became the language of planning, as well as of the military and of the central party; alongside nativisation now came the development of Russian as a common language. Education was increasingly standardised. A particularly important step came in March 1938 when in minority areas the local language remained the main teaching language in primary and secondary schools, but Russian was also made compulsory. A stricter definition of territoriality also meant the disappearance of schools for non-Russian groups living outside their titular regions. More significant still, Russian became the general language of higher education.

The structure of Soviet federalism was elaborated in this period, especially with the adoption of the Stalin Constitution of 1936, but at the same time the power of key sectors were transferred to the centre, with all-union commissariats for internal affairs, agriculture and education, where these had existed earlier at republic level. In March 1938 minority military units were eliminated and Russian became the only official language of the Red Army.

The terror, the war and the nationalities

The Great Terror of 1937 coincided with the beginning of a policy of national deportation (*deportatsiia*). Like so much else, this had its origins in the years before Stalin. The first group deportations had been actually been carried out in Lenin's lifetime, the victims ethnic Russian cossacks. Nevertheless mass deportations of ethnic minorities were a special feature of the Stalin years, condemned by Khrushchev in his 1956 secret speech. The full-blooded Stalinist practice depended on two factors. The first was the development of the secret police, the labour camps and the system of 'special settlers' (*spetsposelentsy*); this last had initially been developed for the deportation of *kulaks* and other peasants after 1929, and it was dekulakisation that had made mass deportation a tool. Furthermore, from 1937 the NKVD powers were greatly extended. The second factor was the external threat in the late 1930s. Imperial Japan invaded north China in July 1937, setting off full-scale war. Korea was then an integral part of Japan, and two months after the war broke out *Sovnarkom* ordered the deportation of the large ethnic Korean minority from the Far Eastern region. Ezhov, head of the secret police, reported to Prime Minister Molotov at the end of October 1937 that the

'resettlement' operation had been carried out: 124 trainloads –
with 36 thousand families, 172 thousand people – shipped off to
the Kazakh and Uzbek SSRs in Central Asia.⁶ The move was not
altogether an irrational reaction, bearing in mind that the total
population of the the Far Eastern region in 1937 was only 2,481
thousand. Significantly this first deportation coincided that
autumn with a number of other ground-breaking NKVD 'mass-
operations' (see Chapter 7). Smaller numbers of ethnic Poles and
Germans were resettled from the western borderlands in the late
1930s.

Deportation is mixed up with another uniquely Stalinist policy, annexation. Although the annexation of the three independent Baltic republics is the best-known, it was numerically less
important than the annexation of eastern Poland (5.7 million
Estonians, Latvians, and Lithuanians versus around 13.4 million
Ukrainians, Belorussians, Jews and Poles). The USSR also
annexed Bessarabia in north west Romania (3.2 million), and
parts of Finland. These changes were partly a reclaiming of territory that had been part of the 1914 Tsarist empire, and in the
case of the Polish gains they at least took Belorussia and the
Ukraine to their ethnic borders (although the opposite was the
case with Bessarabia, where ethnic Romanians were again cut off
from their homeland). The main practical justification was probably military strategy rather than ethnicity or class warfare. The
new territories provided large defensive zones in front of
Leningrad, Minsk and Odessa, which had all been within fifty
miles of the old Finnish, Estonian, Polish and Romanian borders

The annexation of the western regions in 1939–40 was accompanied by new arrests and deportations. Some, like the Korean
deportation or a number of later wartime 'operations', were
essentially 'ethnic cleansing': 390 thousand Poles, for example,
were deported. In other cases, however, the victims of deportation were not whole peoples but rather 'hostile elements' (and
their families), the 'ruling classes' of the formerly independent
states. Large-scale resettlement campaigns struck Romanian
Bessarabia (Moldavia), the western Ukraine and Belorussia and
the Baltic republics on the very eve of the German invasion;
according to NKVD documents 86 thousand people were moved
to Siberia and Kazakstan. There had been a smaller level of
arrests since the June 1940 annexation of the Baltic republics.

One estimate for losses there – including deportation and execution – was 60 thousand for Estonia (including the early wartime
months) and about 35 thousand each for the other two Baltic
republics. The rapid collapse of the western defence zones in
June–July 1941 has to be seen in this context. Large parts of the
local population were hostile to their new Soviet rulers and the
harsh deportation policy was probably counter-productive.

The outbreak of war led to even more extreme measures, this
time deep within the USSR. In 1941 the Volga German ASSR,
near Saratov, was liquidated and some 400 thousand ethnic
Germans were deported to the Siberia and Central Asia. The next
major act in the drama of the Soviet nationalities had to wait
until after Red Army's general counter-offensive. The smaller
minorities settled on the north side of the Caucasus mountains
were the victims. Some of them had long been a thorn in the side
of the central authorities (and would continue to be so into the
1990s), and members of other minorities had collaborated when
the German army held the region from the summer of 1942 to the
beginning of 1943. In October–November 1943, a few months
after the Germans were finally pushed out, the Turkic Karachai
people, settled in the northern part of Stavropol region and
numbering 69 thousand, were deported to the east, and their
autonomous region (the Karachai AO) closed down. In
December 1943 and January 1944, a year after the battle of
Stalingrad, 93 thousand Kalmyks living in the steppe south of
the city were rounded up and deported; the Kalmyk ASSR was
liquidated. Most numerous were the Chechen and Ingush,
whose turn came in March 1944. The Germans had not even
reached the Chechen-Ingush ASSR, but in February–March 1944
Beria presided over the largest of the deportations: some 500
thousand Chechens and Ingush were moved to Central Asia.
According to Beria's own report, some 650,000 Chechen, Ingush,
Karachais and Kalmyks were deported in an operation involving
120,000 internal security troops, to be followed by Balkars and
Meskhetian Turks. Last to be deported from the north Caucasus,
in March–April 1944, were 340 thousand Turkic Balkars (ethni-
cally close to the Karachai) of the Kabardin-Balkar ASSR; they
were also removed from the name of the republic. All of these
deportations involving shipping large number of women, children and old people long distances in crowded freight cars to

barren settlement areas. Many lives were lost: nearly a quarter of 609,000 deported Chechens, Ingush, Karachai and Balkars had died by 1948. Retribution came even more quickly to the Crimean Tatars. The Red Army re-conquered the Crimean peninsula in May 1944 and immediately the Crimean Tatars – 180 thousand in all – were shipped off to Uzbekistan.

There were significant differences between the various wartime deportations. The later ones did not even make a degree of strategic sense, as the Germans by that time were well in retreat to the west. They can only be seen as a grand ethnic punishment or an extreme version of prophylactic counter-insurgency. Some of these nationalities were 'rehabilitated' under Khrushchev, with their republics re-established. The Volga Germans and Crimean Tatars were not, and there grievances remained an issue until the end of Soviet power.

The Stalinist deportation policy did not cease after the victory over Nazi Germany. The Baltic states, western Belorussia, western Ukraine and Moldavia had to be re-sovietised. The wartime turmoil was followed by a substantial guerrilla campaign, with the nationalist 'forest brotherhood' in the Baltic states, especially in Lithuania, and with the Ukrainian Insurgent Army (UPA) in the the western Ukraine. According to one estimate some 50 thousand combatants on either side were killed in the immediate post-war years, although it seems the fighting rapidly tapered off after this. In any event the administration of the regions at various levels was entrusted to carpet-baggers from the east, ethnic Russians or minority officials from the old USSR (i.e. officials from the eastern Ukraine were transferred to the annexed western zone). The largest of the republics was controlled by powerful outsiders. In *de facto* control as supreme party leaders in Kiev were, over the period 1938–53, two ethnic Russians and a Jew (Khrushchev, Mel'nikov, and Kaganovich). The situation in Belorussia was similar. Whatever level of sovietisation had been carried out in the newly-annexed borderlands in 1939–41 was undone by the Germans, and it was only in 1944–50 that these regions were integrated into the Soviet system. Economic and political controls were put in place, which were both cause and effect of the counter-insurgency struggle. In the western Ukraine collectivisation was carried out in late 1948, in the Baltic republics in the spring of 1949 and in western Belorussia in

1952–53. Pre-war and post-war policy combined in a dark period of oppression for the western nationalities. The total numbers
deported for the period 1940–53, as outlined in a secret ministry
of the interior report of December 1965, were some 571 thousand
from the Ukrainian SSR, 61 thousand from the Belorussian SSR,
46 thousand from the Moldavian SSR, 119 thousand from the
Lithuanian SSR, 53 thousand from the Latvian SSR and 33 thousand from the Estonian SSR.

The rise of ethnic Russian nationalism, like the policy of deportation, was carried out against the background of the Second
World War. Significantly, the conflict was called the great war for
the 'fatherland' (*otechestvo*) from the beginning (see document
13). The original 'fatherland war' had been the campaign against
the Napoleonic invasion of 1812. The idea of the fatherland also
had a Soviet pedigree, and was part of an ideological great
retreat from Marx's internationalism. Stalin had made his 1931
speech about the workers now having a fatherland, but the same
point was made in 'socialism in one country' of the mid-1920s
(see documents 1 and 6). Indeed, the fatherland appeared in
some of the appeals Lenin made in the winter of 1917–18 in the
face of another German invasion. Russian patriotism would play
an important part in the war effort of 1941–45. It had a powerful
response from at least the Russian part of the population, especially in the army, and was carefully exploited by the regime.
Stalin was quite explicit about this both at the beginning and the
end of the war. In November 1941 he based Moscow's defence on
Russia's great military heroes – Aleksandr Nevskii, Dmitrii
Donskoi, Minin and Pozharskii, Suvorov and Kutuzov – and
undoubtedly had a respect from Russian national power. The
spirit of first verse of the new national anthem, written in 1943,
was quite different from that of the revolution: 'Unbreakable
union of free republics, the land of Great Rus' has been rallied
together forever! [*Splotila naveki Velikaia Rus'!*] Long live the
Soviet Union, united [*edinyi*] and mighty, created in struggle by
the will of the peoples.'[7] The war was very important, indirectly,
in giving the Communist regime a new kind of legitimacy, as the
defender of the fatherland (or 'motherland' – *rodina*). It built on
other developments, including the emergence of a new (post-
1937) political elite that was more Russian than the revolutionary
one, and on institutions that were dominated by Russians, espe-

cially the Red Army and the military-industrial complex. The emphasis on Russia also came from the way the war unfolded: the Germans over-ran the non-Russian borderland – especially Belorussia and the Ukraine – and the core of the Soviet held-zone was Russian. The three pivotal battles, Moscow, Stalingrad and Kursk were fought on ethnic Russian soil (i.e. within the borders of the Russian federation), but two-thirds of the territory occupied by the Germans belonged to republics peopled by non-Russians.

At the end of Stalin's lifetime anti-semitic propaganda was distributed, and there was a secret trial of Jewish leaders. The 'Doctor's plot' (see Chapter 7) highlighted Jews, and there are undocumented rumours of a planned deportation of the Jews. This campaign seems to have been a product of three factors: the dictator's advancing years, the rise of ethnic Russian nationalism within the post-war elite, and – in the Cold War and after the creation of a Jewish state in Palestine – the identification of the Jews with outside forces. However, anti-semitism was a late development for Stalin. Some of his most important lieutenants – Kaganovich, Iagoda, Mekhlis, Litvinov – had been Jews, and before 1945 the Jews must have seemed especially valuable allies in the ideological struggle with Nazism.

The USSR was not seething with ethnic discontent by the time Stalin died. The apparatus of the secret police, the Communist party's monopoly of power, the demographic, educational, and military advantages of the ethnic Russians, were more than enough to contain ethnic discontent. Deportations and the rise of Russian nationalism were not the undoing of nativisation. Nevertheless there were substantial grievances, which the post-Stalin leadership immediately began to address.

******

Stalinist nationalities policies can be summed up in three Russian words: *korenizatsiia*, *industrializatsiia*, and *deportatsiia*. In the Stalin years these policies coexisted, although there were differences of emphasis. *Korenizatsiia* (nativisation) blossomed, and had its initial impact, in the 1920s. On the other hand, if it is taken to mean encouragement of nationalist territorial identity (in parallel with a 'leading' ethnic Russian culture), recruitment of ethnic minorities to administrative posts (at least to low and intermediate level), and encouragement of primary and secondary education in minority languages, then it continued throughout the Soviet period. Stalinist *industrializatsiia*, if taken to cover the Great Breakthrough as a whole, the social-economic revolution of industrialisation, collectivisation, and the cultural revolution, required *korenizatsiia* as a tool, but at the same time it furthered the cause of 'genuine' nativisation by increasing the urbanised and educated elements within the minorities. The process of Stalinist modernisation was not confined to the 1930s, but also included the post-war economic recovery spurt and the social impact of the war. *Industrializatsiia*, like *korenizatsiia*, would also continue after 1953. *Deportatsiia* takes in the extreme, cruel aspects of the Stalin regime's treatment of the nationalities, not just the main wartime and post-war deportations. In the short term this was effective, but not in the long term; Stalin's successors avoided such extremes, but the memories never disappeared.

The legacy of the Stalin years played its part in the eventual collapse of the USSR in 1991. It was the memory of the Stalinist cruelties of the 1940s, the brutal annexation of the Baltic States and the deportations of whole peoples, like the Crimean Tatars, which opened a Pandora's box of protest in the later 1980s. Also corrosive for a genuine multi-national state was the growth of Russian nationalism. Stalin did not create Russian nationalism, and the predominance of ethnic Russians was not just his whim. Russian nationalism stemmed from followed a range of real factors, including the Russians' numerical superiority, and the appearance of ethnic Russian industrial, cultural and military elites. The Georgian dictator 'only' recognised Russian nationalism as an important force and used it. Meanwhile, the constitutional structure created under Stalin laid the foundations for the transformation of the USSR into the Commonwealth of Independent States. But more important was the modernisation of the nationalities, a by-product of the nativisation which developed from the 1920s. Just as the development of an educated, urbanised population was a direct, and intended, result of the regime's policies, so was the creation of literate and nationally conscious minorities. It was the political consequences of these changes that was unintended.

Notes

1 Stalin, *Sochineniia*, vol. 3[16], pp. 7f.

2 Stalin, 'O politicheskikh zadachakh Universiteta narodov Vostoka [On the political tasks of the University of peoples of the East]', 18 May 1925, *Sochineniia*, vol. 7, p. 138.

3 Stalin, *Sochineniia*, vol. 11, p. 354.

4 G. Simon, *Nationalism and Policy Towards the Nationalities in the Soviet Union* (Boulder CO, 1991), p. 138.

5 Simon, *Nationalism and Policy*, pp. 390–1. The 1939 figure includes territory annexed in 1939–40.

6 The details in this chapter about deportations mostly come from N. F. Bugai, *L. Beriia – I. Stalinu: 'Soglasno Vashemu ukazaniiu ...'* [*L. Beria to J. Stalin: 'In accordance with Your instructions ...'*] (Moscow, 1995). This is the fullest account of Stalinist repression of national minorities; the title comes from the beginning of Beria's reports to Stalin.

7 The medieval name for the lands of the eastern Slavs, which developed into the Russian empire, was *Rus'*. For the full Stalinist text of the anthem, and a more 'poetic' translation, see J. von Geldern and R. Stites (eds), *Mass Culture in Soviet Russia* (Bloomington IN, 1995), p. 406.

6

The two camps:
Stalinism and the outside world

Stalin's 1946 election speech was basically about how Russian military competition with an external enemy had been an 'examination' of the Soviet system. Following Lenin closely, Stalin argued that the 1939–45 war had been no accident: 'the war came about as the inevitable result of the development of world economic and political forces on the basis of modern monopoly capitalism'. This situation also required the continued build-up of heavy industry to 'guarantee' Russia 'against any accidents' (see document 15).[1] The speech was a major public statement about the outside world and about the USSR's relations with it; it prompted the famous 'Long Telegram' of George Kennan, the acting American ambassador, in which he laid out a Cold War counter-strategy of 'containment'.

The Cold War before and after 1945

What were the main developments in Soviet relations with the outside world in the Stalin years? The starting point might be the 1927 war scare, a series of incidents which were taken by Moscow to suggest the imminent danger of open conflict with Britain, France and Poland. This spurred the beginning of the Soviet economic and military build-up. One feature of the 1920s was the Soviet government's unsuccessful attempts to cultivate anti-colonialist allies in China. It was also a time when the Comintern (the Communist International) pursued a more radical policy in Europe, based on a perception of a deepening economic and social crisis.

The events of the early 1930s created for the USSR a situation that was far more dangerous than the 1920s. Japan embarked on expansionist policies, annexing Manchuria from China in 1931 and threatening the sparsely-populated Russian Pacific coast. In Germany the Great Depression led to the victory not of the German Communists, but of Hitler. The Nazis were doubly dangerous – both expansionist and anti-Communist. Moscow's belated response, at the start of 1934, was a change to co-operation with the enemies of Germany and Japan under a policy of 'collective security'. The USSR signed treaties of mutual assistance with France and Czechoslovakia in 1935, and gave military aid to the Spanish republic. In the east the Chinese Nationalist government was given military and diplomatic support after the Sino-Japanese broke out in 1937. The Comintern, for its part, was given a new 'line', supporting within capitalist countries the anti-Fascist 'popular front' coalitions of liberals, socialists and communists.

This phase came to an abrupt and shocking end in August 1939, with the German–Soviet non-aggression pact. The pact led not only to a pro-German neutrality in the 'European War', but also to extensive economic co-operation and to the partition of Poland and other parts of eastern Europe between Germany and the USSR. The Soviet–Japanese non-aggression pact of April 1941 also involved an attempt to come to appease an expansionist enemy. In Europe the new policy endured less than two years and ended with the the German surprise attack in June 1941 (see document 13). The immediate effect was another diplomatic about-turn, this time involuntary, with the formation of the 'Grand Alliance' with the British (and later the Americans). Moscow played down the cause of international revolution; the Comintern itself was dissolved in 1943. Inter-Allied co-operation appeared for a time to include real negotiation and compromise; Stalin was personally involved with Allied leaders in meetings in Moscow and at the summit conferences in Teheran (December 1943), Yalta (February 1945) and Potsdam (July 1945).

This relationship broke down after the defeat of the common enemy and was followed by the Cold War. Moscow failed to make a working agreement with America and Britain over

Germany or over the extent of Soviet influence in eastern Europe. By 1947 Washington had become committed to containment. Over the next two years hostility escalated from rhetoric, through diplomatic maneuvres and alliance-building, to a new military build up. The Americans pushed through a division of Germany, and the Soviets brought eastern Europe under direct Communist control. A new international Communist organisation, the Cominform (the Communist Information Bureau), was established, and it excluded the divergent views of Tito's Yugoslav Communists (see document 17). In the late summer of 1949 the USSR tested its first atomic bomb. With the victory of the Chinese Communists in 1948–49 Moscow's interest in Asia was revived, and the now global Cold War was intensified by Stalin's sponsorship of the North Korean invasion of South Korea in 1950 (see document 18). Attempts to improve East–West relations came only with Stalin's death.

Such were the basic events. No historiographical debate concerning the Stalin years has been longer running than the attempt to find 'the sources of Soviet conduct', as Kennan entitled the Long Telegram's sequel, a famous 1947 article in the journal *Foreign Affairs*. Historians differ fundamentally about the nature of Stalin's relations with the outside world, and especially about the origins of the Cold War, which set the pattern for forty years of world history. One division is between the traditionalists (or 'Cold Warriors'), who stressed agressive Soviet Communism, and the 'revisionists' of the 1960s, who blamed more the western side and saw Soviet policy as reactive. This argument is based on very different perceptions of Stalin and the Soviet leadership. For some traditionalists Stalin was a revolutionary, the conscious continuer of Lenin's (and Trotsky's) world revolutionary policies. Those at the other extreme, the revisionists, shared Trotsky's estimation of Stalin and his comrades ('the bureaucracy') as conservatives, people for whom socialism in one country meant ignoring revolutions in other countries. In this second view Stalin was a man who 'betrayed' the international revolution as much as the Russian one; for historical revisionists it made Russia a 'force of stability' and Stalin a 'normal statesman' with whom the west missed the chance to 'do business'.[2] It is, of course, possible to see Stalin as both a betrayer of socialism *and* as an agressive Russian imperialist.

Did Stalin make foreign policy? The consensus of new research is that from the discussion of the Chinese question in 1927 to decision-making over Germany and Korea in 1952 Stalin was very much dominant. In the 1930s Stalin left more tactical latitude to Litvinov, the head of the foreign affairs commissariat (*Narkomindel*), but from 1939 he installed his first lieutenant, Molotov, as people's commissar. Late in his life Stalin maintained an interest in world affairs when he had delegated many aspects of domestic policy to others, it became almost an old man's hobby. As in other areas (economic planning, persecution of 'enemies', culture) there was some room for internal policy discussion, but Stalin kept the last word;

One of the central arguments of this book is that Stalin was a 'true-believer' in Marxism-Leninism. The 'world view' naturally applied to the world outside, not only to Russia. From Marx came key notions: a crisis-ridden capitalism heading for collapse, the centrality of the class struggle and the falsehood of the parliamentarism. From Lenin came others: first, a rapacious imperialism and, as a consequence, the inevitability of wars and, second, Bolshevik central party direction. The distrust of the outside world was not, for Stalin and a generation of Communist leaders, an abstraction. The experience of the First World War and the civil war had reinforced it; Russia had been ground first between the two European power blocs and then, after November 1918, had suffered blockade and intervention by the victorious Allies. For Moscow there was a dual division, on the one hand between capitalist states and socialist ones and on the other between rival capitalist states. Both divisions threatened wars that might involve the USSR, and both required massive Soviet military strength. The capitalist–socialist rivalry was, however, the primary one for Stalin throughout his years in power. The famous notion of the 'two camps' is usually associated with Andrei Zhdanov and a speech made in mid-1947, but the concept belonged to Stalin, and it harked back to an article of the same name that Stalin wrote in February 1919. 'The world,' he said then, 'has definitely and irrevocably split into two camps: the camp of imperialism and the camp of socialism'.[3]

Within this 'two-camps' world-view there was room for manoeuvre, and the model was a policy first laid out in the winter of 1917–18. Lenin then argued not for a direct revolutionary onslaught against world capitalism, but for exploitation of the divisions between the two imperialist alliances and an orientation towards one of them; the result was the separate peace with the German-led Central Powers. This diplomatic orientation to one side or the other continued in the inter-war years. The 1922 Treaty of Rapallo kept Russia diplomatically close to Germany up to 1933, and a similar orientation followed in 1939–41. At other times Moscow sided with the anti-German bloc, in 1934–39 and – involuntarily – from 1941. Such manoeuvres depended on the continuing existence of two rival imperialist blocs and it could be argued that the total defeat of Germany and Japan made this strategy impossible. But even in the pre-war years it was the socialist–imperialist division that was most important. It was difficult for Stalinist Russia to have normal friendly relations with any other state. The two camps world view of the Soviet leaders makes unconvincing the argument that Stalin secretly hoped for close relations with Hitler from the mid-1930s or even trusted him in 1939–41. It was Hitler who pushed for the 1939 non-aggression pact, and Stalin who grudgingly agreed to it. For the same reason in 1934–39 the top Soviet leadership, if not Litvinov, saw the British and the French as, at best, fellow travellers. The Kremlin may well have welcomed the outbreak of war in 1939 as a means of weakening both 'imperialist blocs'. The Grand Alliance of 1941 was forced on the USSR by Hitler, and as the war came to a close Stalin did not believe that friendship – or even a condominium – with Washington and London would be a sensible substitute for installing Communist governments, at least in neighbouring countries.[4]

It was hard for the USSR to establish genuinely close relationships, even within the socialist 'camp', with the Communist-led governments set up from 1945. The expulsion of radical Yugoslavia from the camp in 1948 was the most striking incident, but there were trials of Communist leaders in other satellites. There was even a latent dispute with China, as witnessed by Mao Zedong's wary negotiations with Stalin in 1949–50. The Communist Party of the Soviet Union's (CPSU) pre-war relations with the non-ruling Communist parties had never been one of equals, and at least since 1920 the international Communist movement had been thoroughly 'Bolshevised' – brought under the control of the Russian party.

The two camps world view was not just about polarity. Also highly important were two other factors. The first was the 'correlation of forces', the relative potential strength of the two camps. The second was how actively or passively either camp pursued the latent hostilities. In terms of potential strength there was in the late 1920s and early 1930s a belief, not confined to Moscow, that capitalism was on the edge of collapse; this was one of the reasons why the Nazis were underestimated in 1930–33. On the other hand, the potential danger facing the Soviet Union in the 1930s was considerable. It was an isolated socialist country facing four fundamentally unfriendly major powers (Britain, France, Germany and Japan) and several unfriendly smaller ones (especially Poland and Romania). Until the end of the 1930s the correlation of forces was such that the USSR lacked the ability, even on paper, to defend its territorial integrity against a worst-case coalition attack. The correlation of forces was radically different by the end of 1945. Germany and Japan, and Germany's allies, had been eliminated; Britain and France had been seriously weakened; the borders of the USSR had been pushed westwards and the Red Army occupied territories even beyond those they had occupied in 1939–40. The United States had, however, moved from the diplomatic periphery to the centre of the imperialist bloc, with influence both in Europe and Asia, and the American atomic bomb was a new and dangerous factor. Meanwhile the foreign Communist parties were now a more important force than they had been 1939, thanks to their role in the Resistance and the temporary bankruptcy of countervailing conservative forces. Another factor that Soviet leaders put in their calculations was the economic stability of the imperialist camp and, based on both Marxism-Leninism and the experience of the Great Depression, they expected the capitalist world to be crippled by further economic crises. By mid-1950 the correlation of forces had turned even more in favour of the socialist camp with the creation of reliable Communist governments on the western periphery, Mao's victory in China and the test of the Soviet atomic bomb.

The intentions of the two camps were harder to weigh up than their relative potential strength. The Soviet perception, or misperception, of the intentions of the capitalist world was crucial to its foreign policy, and was so from the beginning of Soviet

Russia. The 1927 war scare exemplified this. Distrust of the British, French and Poles made it impossible to form an effective anti-German grouping, and their resolve in 1939 was underestimated. In 1945 there was little trust in Americans and British intentions, and by February 1946 Stalin was openly talking about the danger of 'accidents' (see document 15). By August 1947 the two camps perception was publicly made the centre of policy. This was to go on until 1956, and perhaps even until 1988 when Gorbachev brought in the 'new thinking' on foreign policy.

Why did the USSR read the external world's intentions in this light? Partly it came from Stalin's personal paranoia. He trusted no-one, either within the USSR or beyond its borders. He was surrounded by men who shared his views. Kennan, in his 'Long Telegram' mode, made much of a traditional Russian xenophobia, and there was more than a grain of truth in this. Marxism-Leninism predisposed the party leadership to assume capitalist hostility. Most of the veterans of the foreign commissariat were in 1937–38 purged and replaced by ignorant and inflexible young men. It may also have been the case that active enemies were required to justify internal policies of industrialisation and terror. All of this could be superimposed on a real history of Russian conflict, a most significant chapter of which was the German invasion.

The intentions of the socialist camp also counted. If those intentions were seen as hostile, then the chances of productive East–West relations were poor. Soviet attempts at tactical flexibility were always marred by inconsistencies, not all of Stalin's making. Throughout the Soviet period – except perhaps 1942–44 – Moscow appeared to be trying to combine conventional balance-of-power diplomacy and world revolution. In the 1920s and 1930s the Comintern existed alongside the foreign commissariat, in the 1940s the Cominform existed alongside the lukewarm Soviet attempts to normalise relations (this duality long-outlived the Stalin era and spoiled détente in the 1970s). Stalin may have attempted, for tactical reasons, to move towards a more moderate policy in 1934, 1941, 1945 and perhaps in 1949, but this was negated by what had happened earlier.[5] It was a vicious circle. Fear of the outside made Moscow take extraordinary measures to guarantee its security; those measures themselves fanned the fears of outsiders. Stalin's successors were left with a territorial legacy which locked them into thirty years of tension with the West. Stalin's two camps served as a self-fulfilling prophecy.

The Great Fatherland War

The most extreme feature of Stalinist Russia's relation with the outside world was the Soviet–German war. Its history can be divided into two halves, before and after the winter of 1942–43; the turning point being the Battle of Stalingrad. Regarding the first half of the war there are two central questions: why did the Red Army suffer such extraordinary defeats and why were the Nazis not able to achieve their objectives? Regarding the second half the questions are: how far was the eventual triumph based on the Soviet system, as Stalin boasted in 1946, and how far was it based on other factors?

The catastrophe of 1941–42 was, in absolute terms of losses of territory, personnel and equipment, the worst defeat ever suffered in any war. Within four months the Russians had given up territory to a line running from Leningrad to west of Moscow, which they would not cross again until the summer of 1943. It is now reported that during 1941 the Soviet forces lost 3.1 million personnel, captured, killed, and missing; about 600 thousand a month for five months.[6] Some 11 thousand Soviet aircraft were lost in combat in 1941. Tank losses numbered 20 thousand, and losses of guns and mortars were 101 thousand. The northern and central parts of the front were stabilised after the Soviets stopped the initial onslaught at the Battle of Moscow (December 1941–January 1942), but the German's spring 1942 offensive broke through the Soviet line in the south. The Germans recaptured the Donbas mining region and advanced in two prongs east to Stalingrad on the Volga, and south east towards the oil wells of the Caucasus. Soviet losses in 1942 were again phenomenal: 3.3 million personnel killed, missing, and captured, and a further 4.1 million wounded and sick. Equipment losses were another 15 thousand tanks, 108 thousand guns and mortars and 9 thousand aircraft.

This disaster had various explanations. The impact of the purges is less easy to assess than it once seemed. New information suggests that the extent of the army purge has been exaggerated, or at least must be seen in the context of the simultaneous expansion of the army. In 1937 the ground forces lost 19 thousand out of a total of 142 thousand commanders and commissars, and in 1938–39 a similar number, so the command staff were 'only' decimated – losing about one in ten, to correctly use that highly appropriate term from the Roman Army.[7] Altogether 34 thousand commanders and commissars from the ground and air forces were discharged, of which 12 thousand had been reinstated by May 1940. At that time the command staff of the army were increasing rapidly, to a total of 282 thousand in 1939. Red Army officer combat losses in 1941 – 203 thousand. – must have had much more impact. The Red Army was not in any event leaderless after 1937–38; a large pool of qualified officers survived, and there was an element of top-level continuity in the person of the defence commissar, Marshal Voroshilov. The victorious army-group, army, corps and division commanders of 1943–45 were regiment and battalion commanders in 1937–38. However, even if the losses had amounted to less than ten per cent the victims were some of the most senior and experienced commanders – 60 of 67 corps commanders, 136 of 199 division commanders, 221 of 397 brigade commanders, and half the regimental commanders. The secondary effects of the purges were also important. Independent thought was replaced by strong caution. Discipline suffered. Equipment modernisation was badly affected. Finally, the Red Army purges made Britain and France discount the USSR as a military partner in 1938 and 1939 and, even more fatal, made Hitler more ready to attack. The purges had undermined the deterrent value of the Red Army.

The disaster of 1941–42 did not happen because Stalin's Russia was unprepared for war. The leadership had been acutely conscious of an international danger since at least 1927. Armaments programmes formed a large part of the Five-year plans from the beginning. In contrast, Germany did not start to re-arm until 1935. The Red Army had expanded from 560 thousand in 1925 (partly militia), to 1.5 million in mid-1938, 4.5 million in February 1940, and 5 million in June 1941. As the favoured child of the regime it received lavish amounts of new equipment. In the early and middle 1930s Stalin's government endorsed new military concepts which paralleled radical economic and social policies. The Soviets pioneered specialist tank forces. In 1941 the

USSR had 23 thousand tanks, 337 thousand guns and mortars and 20 thousand combat aircraft. The Soviet forces had also by this time been tested in battle. In the late 1930s Soviet airmen and soldiers had more chances to try out their modern equipment than their counterparts from any other country, in Spain, China and in border battles with the Japanese. This combat experience continued even after the outbreak of the 'European War'. Remarkable as it may seem, the German army had actually suffered lower losses before June 1941 than had the 'neutral' Red Army (above all, 126 thousand in the abortive invasion of Finland, the so-called Winter War). Far from being complacent Stalin, prompted by the Finnish fiasco and Hitler's astonishing lightning victories in Poland and France, presided over a year of frantic reorganisation in the Red Army by the time of Barbarossa. The annexation of territories in the west in 1939–40 was part of this military strategic preparation, deepening the line of defence and securing strategic points on the Baltic and Black Sea.

The preparations of the Red Army also included, in the spring of 1941, a secret transfer of forces from the eastern military districts and the call-up of some 800 thousand reservists. This has been seen by a minority of historians as Soviet preparation for a premptive attack.[8] Some extreme revisionists have used this to justify Hitler's attack; other historians have suggested that a pre-emptive attack would have been the best Soviet course. Neither is convincing. Hitler's decision had nothing to do with any concrete knowledge of a Soviet attack. It is relevant that the Red Army in the 1930s (as after 1945) had an offensive strategy, which envisaged taking the war into the enemy's territory from the outset, using highly mobile forces and resolving the struggle quickly. This was part of the carefully thought out build-up of mechanised forces and aviation in the 1930s which, far from being Stalin's concept, owed much to the purged Marshal Tukhachevskii. But in 1941 a pre-emptive attack was not a practical proposition. The Red Army showed shortcomings against much less effective enemies in offensive operations in eastern Poland and Finland before 1940 and could not carry off a prolonged offensive in the spring of 1942, even after a year's wartime experience. In fact Russia got the worst of both worlds, because concentration on an inappropriate offensive strategy meant that not enough thought was given to the strategy and tactics of defence or to a long war.

Stalin has been repeatedly condemned for allowing the Red Army to be caught by surprise on 22 June, despite many German overflights and warnings from intelligence sources and so on. Although he must bear ultimate responsibility, he was hardly, as we have seen, blindly oblivious to the threat of war. Several factors seem to have been operating. First, the Germans were able to mask much of their build-up. Second, Moscow assumed that Hitler was too rational to try to fight a war on two fronts – to take on Russia before eliminating Britain; that this was strategic suicide was confirmed in 1943–45. Third, the Russians interpreted the part of the German build-up that they knew about as diplomatic pressure – bluff – rather than preparations for actually fighting a war. Finally, there was an assumption that the initial period of the war would include, like previous wars, a period of mobilisation. Russia had also not carried out a full mobilisation, although some steps had been taken; hundreds of thousands of reservists were captured *en route* to their units. It is also worth recalling, however, that in the July 1914 crisis it was Tsarist Russia's decision to begin mobilisation that helped precipitate general war, and that may have been a consideration for Stalin and the high command in 1941. Whatever its cause, the surprise of 22 June had the most devastating consequences. Losses in the early weeks, especially in aircraft destroyed on the ground and forward-based tank units, could not be made good for two years. Once the Red Army began its long headlong withdrawal it found it impossible to co-ordinate counter-attacks on the open and mobile battlefield. The precipitate retreat could not be stopped until the enemy ran out of supplies. The Soviet Union had not mobilised many of its its reservists, which allowed the Germans to achieve parity between the attacking forces and those on hand on the Soviet western border.

Another factor in the early defeats was poor Soviet military leadership. Despite his brilliant civil war career Marshal Budennyi commanded badly the defence of Ukraine, ending in the Kiev fiasco (the encirclement of hundreds of thousands of Soviet troops at Kiev). Marshal Voroshilov was little more successful in front of Leningrad. The high command had wrongly assumed that the main attack would be in the south, in the Ukraine, rather than in Belorussia. They would make the opposite mistake in the spring of 1942, assuming that the main German thrust would be against Moscow rather than the south.

Beyond military factors, there were diplomatic ones. The USSR suffered so heavily because it fought on its own. Even if the Red Army had been on high alert on 22 June 1941, with troops in their forward positions and aircraft dispersed, even if full mobilisation of reserves had been carried out, the USSR would still have been isolated. As Moscow would complain, there was no Second Front, but this was due not to the duplicity of London and Washington. The costs of the purges had been high. Foreign states had seen the USSR as critically weakened in 1930s, and in turn Stalin's 'cunning' policy of the Nazi–Soviet pact period allowed Germany to knock France out of the war and drive the British army out of north west Europe. It does not matter that Stalin had not – any more than much of the German high command – expected the collapse of France in six weeks; his diplomacy facilitated that outcome.

Given all this, why was Stalin's Russia not destroyed? After all, the German high command largely succeeded in their original intention of destroying the Red Army on the frontiers. Survival had little to do with Russia's allies. The fighting in the west was still limited. Rommel's famous Afrika Korps had at its peak strength three German divisions: 152 divisions were employed in the June attack on Russia. As for Lend-lease, only a trickle reached the Soviet-German front in 1941–42. More telling as a factor was the Soviet system itself. There was a lavishly supported propaganda machine. The role of the pre-war 'voluntary' organisations for paramilitary training should not be underestimated; the most important, *Osoaviakhim*, had 13 million members by 1940. As we saw in Chapter 5, Russian patriotism became the keynote from the beginning. There was a large apparatus of internal control, and any possible political opposition had been 'repressed' in the purges (see document 12). Severe punishments were applied to incompetents and deserters. The commander of the Western army group, General Pavlov, was shot after the first great encirclement. Various draconian orders were put forward, most famously the 'Not one step back!' order of July 1942, with its punishment battations and blocking detachments (see document 14). During the whole war some 994 thousand Soviet personnel were 'condemned', including 376 thousand for desertion. The extreme was the deportation of whole ethnic groups for supposed collaboration.

Stalin kept his nerve. Contrary to some accounts, he did not go into a state of shock on 22 June. Although it was probably regrettable to him that Hitler had torn up the non-aggression pact, the Soviet leader did not expect military catastrophe. Details have now been published of his hectic round of meetings in the war's first week. It does seem to be true that Stalin had a personal crisis a week or so later, retreating to his *dacha* (country house), when the enormity of Pavlov's defeat in Belorussia became clear: the first of the great encirclements had trapped three field armies, 430 thousand men, west of Minsk. But even then he recovered quickly and within two or three days made his famous radio address to his 'brothers and sisters' (see document 13). Stalin had associated himself with the high command at the start, as commissar of defence and head of the Supreme High Command. He was not a great commander. His orders to hold ground had devastating effects in 1941. Even at the early part of 1942, after the successful Battle of Moscow, he ignored his military advisers and committed the Red Army to a general counter-offensive which gained ground but failed to destroy any significant part of the Germany army. In the long term his taking direct responsibility for the war effort probably stiffened Soviet resistance. He stayed in Moscow during the October 1941 crisis and reviewed the 7 November parade; these were vital psychological gestures. Even the stand-fast orders had their place when the Red Army was unable to conduct an effective mobile defence and panic was the greatest danger.

Soviet survival, of course, had much to do with the defensive battles fought by the Russian army. It was actually deployed in depth in June 1941, with a second general group of forces being prepared on the line of the Dvina and Dnepr rivers. The Battle of Smolensk helped stop the German main force, Army Group Centre, for two months in July–September 1941, if at the cost of 486 thousand Red soldiers. And Operation 'Uranus', the final trap which closed shut around the German 6th Army at Stalingrad and ended the first period of the war, was a military classic.

The underlying factors behind Soviet survival were, however, geographic and demographic. The geography worked in favour of the Soviets. The German army advanced 600 miles to the approaches to Moscow, but was nowhere near dominating the whole country. Gor'kii, the 'Soviet Detroit', and Kuibyshev (Samara), the replacement capital, were, respectively, 250 and 500 miles east. It was another thousand miles to the new arsenals of the central Urals. Hitler was blamed by his generals for indecision, shifting the emphasis to the south in July–August 1941, rather than going for Moscow, but this option was probably as good as any other. In 1941 the German army had the ability to take whatever it wanted in the western USSR, but it could not take *everything*. The weather was also a famous part of the campaign, again working in the Soviet's favour. Snow neutralised German technical and organisational advantages at Moscow and Stalingrad, but as important was the autumn and spring mud – the *rasputitsa* – which made vehicle movement so difficult. It was not simply a question of distance, but also of a poor transport system. The USSR had a population of about 200 million in June 1941, and most of the core who remained, even after the great defeats of 1941 were the ethnic Russians in the Moscow–Volga–Urals area. The population advantage, plus the Soviet pre-war preparations, meant that it was possible for the Russians to field a huge army and, if necessary, defend the country by strength of numbers. It was the ability to mobilise new formations which eventually stopped the German offensives. In this would lie both the German failure and the enormously high cost which the Russian paid for it.

In the face of the distances involved and the size of the Soviet population, the initial German forces were weak. Of the 'armoured fist' of 3,100 German tanks in June 1941 a quarter were small ten-tonners and another quarter were captured Czechoslovak light tanks. By way of comparison, by the time the Soviets returned to this border area in 1944 their tank force consisted of something like 3,000 heavy (45 ton) tanks, 11,000 medium (32 ton) T-34s, and 16,000 light tanks and self-propelled guns. In the end Hitler was drawn deeper and deeper into Russia until, in November 1942, and over-extended, the jaws snapped closed around Paulus's Sixth Army in Stalingrad. The flanks of the swollen front had had to be covered by Romanian and Hungarian divisions.

The German generals later blamed Hitler's mistakes. This was certainly a factor at several levels. The turn to the Ukraine in August 1941 was probably not a mistake, but prolonging the November campaign against Moscow was, as was the over-ambitious southern campaign in 1942 (Stalingrad *and* the Caucasus), and above all the failure to pull back from Stalingrad at the moment of the November 1942 encirclement. In fact, Hitler's campaign in Russia was based on political-ideological premises rather than military-strategic ones, and in this Hitler was little different from his 'professional' military advisers. In conventional terms the conquest of Russia appeared impossible – indeed, it was impossible. It only seemed possible on the assumption that Stalin's Russia would collapse politically. The paradox was that the Nazis also proved incapable, because they were Nazis, of conducting a serious *political* campaign against Stalinist Russia, winning over anti-Stalin Russians or the Soviet minorities. The Germans' harsh treatment of the population of the occupied regions meant they could get little active support, had they wanted it. Some 2.8 million forced labourers (*Ostarbeiters*) were conscripted from the USSR. The Germans treated the vast number of prisoners they took in 1941 extreme-ly poorly; altogether 3.5 million of 5.7 apparently died in captiv-ity, more than half the size of the Jewish Holocaust. Even if the behaviour of the occupying Germans had been more calculated to 'win hearts and minds' the Soviet Union had a highly devel-oped propaganda system. Winning support in the conquered territories became even more difficult for the Germans once they had moved beyond the belt of territory only recently annexed by Moscow.

The battle of Stalingrad was followed by the victorious years of 1943–45. In July 1943 came the Battle of the Kursk, in which the Red Army stopped the Hitler's main summer offensive. This was followed by Soviet operations named after Tsarist military heroes, 'Kutuzov', 'Rumiantsev' and 'Suvorov', which pushed the Germans back to the borders of the Russian federation and out of the eastern Ukraine. In 1944 Red Army offensives, the 'ten Stalinist crushing blows', made deep advances along the length of the enormous front, the most crushing of which was a blow with another patriotic name, 'Bagration'; in June–August 1944 it broke the back of the Army Group Centre, and pushed the Germans out of Belorussia and half way across Poland to the outskirts of Warsaw. The Axis satellites, Romania, then Bulgaria and Finland, changed sides. The dream of the Tsars – and in a sense of Lenin – was realised as Russian armies for the first time broke successfully across the 1939 and 1914 borders and into the Balkans. In the late winter of 1944–45 they entered into Hungary and western Poland and finally, in the spring, the Reich itself. Berlin fell to the Russians in May 1945.

The Soviet system came into its own in the second half of the war. As we saw in Chapter 2, the victory was in the end a victory for the Stalinist economic campaigns of the 1930s. After initial problems caused by loss of territory came the phoenix of Soviet war production in 1943. After 1942, also, the Western allies' contribution was important for weapons, for supplies and for strategic raw materials; American lorries were crucial for the Soviet mobile operations in 1943–45, for example. But the USSR succeeded on its own in overtaking Germany in the quantity of production in basic items like tanks, artillery, small arms and aircraft. The resources lavished in the 1930s on technical education and military research and development paid off, with the development of equipment that was as good as that of the Germans, in some case superior, and in all cases available in larger numbers.

Against this background of advantages, the Soviet Union had also developed more effective armed forces. It both rebuilt on the foundations surviving under the ruins of the pre-1941 system and created something new. A great deal was learned from the enemy; as Stalin candidly told Mao Zedong, 'the Soviet Army in the struggle with the first-class-armed Germany army received experience in contemporary warfare and turned into an up-to-date well-equipped army'.[9] The command system effectively combined the various branches of service – infantry, artillery, tanks, tactical aircraft – in a way that the Germans had first achieved on a smaller scale in 1939–41. The Red Army developed the ability both to concentrate forces at the decisive point and to co-ordinate attacks over a very broad front. 'Deep battle', the 1930s vision of the purged Marshal Tukhachevskii, was realised by the Guards Tank armies in 1943–45. It is not yet clear how far the Russians benefited from signals intelligence ('Ultra', and so on) but they proved effective in *maskirovka*, 'deception' both at strategic and tactical level. The political marshals had been sidelined. A corps of highly effective commanders emerged, all of them pre-war middle rank officers, of whom Marshal Zhukov is the best known. In the army as a whole there was a growing decentralisation of power as local commanders, now tested in battle, were given greater initiative. Stalin's role in all this has to be disentangled from his own myth of the 'great war leader' and Khrushchev's anti-myth of Stalin the military dilettante. He became more flexible after Stalingrad (although whether this flexibility was cause or result of the Red Army's improved performance is open to debate). He was more prepared to accept the advice of his military commanders. Western diplomats and commands who met Stalin at conferences were certainly very impressed by how well briefed he was. In early 1943 he took the title of Marshal, and in 1945 the even grander one of *Generalissimus*.

The last three years were not, even with this developed military-economic system, ones of unmixed success. More is becoming known, for example, about the failure of Operation 'Mars' in the winter of 1942–43, which might have created a second Stalingrad west of Moscow; it appears to have received more resources than the Stalingrad operation itself.[10] A number of Soviet offensives in 1943 and 1944 were stalled. More significantly, the years of victory were very costly. Operation 'Bagration' destroyed the German Army Group Centre but it cost the lives of 179 thousand Soviet soldiers. The Battle of Berlin, a three-week operation fought in the last days of the war, brought Soviet losses of 78 thousand. The figures for killed, missing and captured were 2.3 million in 1943, 1.8 million in 1944, and 800 thousand for the five months of 1945. Equipment losses in Europe in 1943–45 totalled 61 thousand tanks, 109 thousand guns and mortars, and 26 thousand aircraft; tank and aircraft losses were substantially higher than in 1941–42. The Red Army did become more sparing in its use of manpower – it was in fact actually running short – but in comparison with the Western allies it was still profligate.

As well as achieving victory only at a very high price, the complete defeat of Nazi Germany in 1943–45 involved a number of factors beyond the Stalinist system. The demographic factor is vitally important in both the defensive and offensive periods. By the spring of 1943 the Russians had 5.8 million combat troops and 6,000 tanks; Germany army strength was 2.7 million men and 1,300 tanks – a third the number of tanks with which they had started in 1941. The problems of the Germans became greater as they had to devote more and more to other theatres. Indeed, given general numerical imbalance, the question might be posed as to why it took the Soviets so long to get to Berlin. The German economy was more geared to 'total war' after the winter of 1941–42, but by then nothing could have been done to cope quantitatively with Soviet, British and, especially, American production. It was also too late for Germany to change its image in the occupied territories, even had Hitler been willing to change his policies.

The German effort was now fragmented by fighting on other fronts. A land front mortally serious to the Reich only developed in the West after June 1944, with the Normandy invasion, but the Germans had had to commit significant quantities of high quality troops and aircraft to North Africa and Italy in 1943 and 1944. The British and Americans effectively knocked Hitler's major European ally, Fascist Italy, out of the war in the summer of 1943. While the Soviet navy played only a limited coastal role, the western allies devoted massive resources to keeping control of the seas and blockading Germany. The British and American strategic bombing campaign also had an important impact on the eastern front, dislocating the German industrial production and forcing the Germans to put their main fighter force into air defence and to shift much of artillery production into anti-aircraft guns.

'Victors may and must be judged', Stalin told his 'electors' in 1946. The Great Patriotic War was ultimately a great victory. Stalin's Russia drove the Nazi invaders out of the country, broke the German army and 'liberated' eastern Europe. Stalin used the memory of the war to rally popular support, as did Khrushchev and Brezhnev after him. Even Boris Yeltsin erected a statue of Marshal Zhukov in Red Square. For the ordinary people of Russia, at least for the survivors, what happened was indeed a victory. But the victors can be judged much more harshly. The war was no vindication of the Stalinist system. Military competence is not measured by the number of one's own troops who are sacrificed. It took the USSR three and half years and some ten million soldiers to defeat a state half its size; German military dead on all fronts numbered less than half the number of Soviet dead. In this sense Russia lost the Great Patriotic War. America and Britain fought a different, technological war, one involving immense naval and strategic air forces that were absent from the Soviet war effort and which cost a fraction of the losses in human life. America became a world power at the cost of 274 thousand combatants, and Britain reprieved her empire at a cost of 300 thousand combatants and 50 thousand civilians.

******

The war of 1941–45 was in many respects the centrepiece of the Stalin years. The Stalinist state was in many respects ideally suited to fighting Second World War, but was also fundamentally incapable of good relations with outside countries. Did the policies of Lenin and Stalin bring the German threat upon Russia? This ultimate question is basically unanswerable, but the world would probably have been a dangerous place in the 1930s, even without Stalin and the USSR. Soviet external policy contains another paradox. Soviet Russia 'defeated' Nazi Germany, expanded the socialist 'camp', and turned the correlation of forces in its favour, but the overall assessment of Stalinist foreign policy can be that it was grotesquely unsuccessful, and not just from the perspective of the collapse of Communist eastern Europe in 1989. There was no revolution in other countries. Stalinist policy, locked inflexibly into the two camps perspective, resulted even in the short term in precisely the things Stalin had feared. These included the Nazi invasion thrown against an isolated Russia, a large post-war American presence on the periphery, an economically – and later militarily – powerful West Germany, military alliances arrayed against Russia and the peacetime rearmament of the United States. Victory confirmed habits which eventually bankrupted the country. The two camps paradigm was critical for spoiling Communist relations with the outside world and led Russia into international catastrophe. But its importance did not end there, as it helps explain the most extraordinary aspect of Stalinism: the terror.

Notes

1   Stalin, *Sochineniia*, vol. 3[16], pp. 2, 20. Gorbachev used the same

metaphor of the war as an examination – which the system passed – in his speech forty-one years later on the anniversary of the revolution: M. S. Gorbachev, *Izbrannye rechi i stat'i* [*Selected Speeches and Articles*], vol. 5, (Moscow, 1988), p. 405.

2   The newest version of the revolutionary Stalin is in R. C. Raack, *Stalin's Drive to the West, 1838–1945: The Origins of the Cold War* (Standford, 1995). Stalin the 'normal statesman' tends not to appear in specialist works any more, but the classic presentation of the latter view is G. Kolko, *The Politics of War* (New York, 1968).

3   See document 17. The original version is I. V. Stalin, 'Dvia lageria', *Sochineniia*, vol. 4, p. 232.

4   This is one way in which the present interpretation differs from the new work of Zubok and Pleshakov, who maintain that in 1945–47 Stalin sought to avoid confronation: V. Zubok and C. Pleshakov, *Inside the Kremlin's Cold War* (Cambridge MA, 1996).

5   On this see the classic work of M. Shulman, *Stalin's Foreign Policy Reappraised* (Cambridge 1963).

6   Military statistics in this chapter are based mainly on G. F. Krivosheev (ed.), *Soviet Casualties and Combat Losses in the Twentieth Century* (London, 1997). Figures for personnel 'losses' here and later are for what Russian statisticians call 'permanent' losses, i.e. those who were killed, died of wounds or illnesses, captured, or went missing. Total casualties – including wounded – were much higher.

7   On the army purge see R. Reese, *Stalin's Reluctant Soldiers* (Lawrence KA, 1996).

8   The best known version is V. Suvorov, *Icebreaker: Who Started the Second World War?* (London, 1990).

9   *Cold War International History Project Bulletin*, 6–7, p. 51.

10   D. Glantz and J. House, *When Titans Clashed* (Lawrence KA, 1995), pp. 136–9.

7

The terror:
Stalinism and repression

Much of what happened in the Stalin years was easy enough to understand. The system's policies logically followed the Marxist ideology of Russia's new rulers. These policies were not uniquely 'Stalinist', as they corresponded to earlier and later Soviet developments, between 1917 and 1929 and between 1953 and 1991. Other developments were not even uniquely Russian or Communist. State-sponsored economic modernisation has been a standard feature of the twentieth-century world. Stalinist Russia was certainly not the only modern country which was not a multi-party, parliamentary democracy, nor was it the only state to throw up a dictator. It was not alone – especially in the 1930s – in seeing the international environment as unusually dangerous.

One feature of the Stalin years, however, sets them apart. That was the level of violence inflicted on the Russian population by their own government, especially through the means of the secret police and vast penal system that we know as the GULAG. There is no one term adequate for the execution of a million people, the death by criminal state neglect of even more in the penal system, and the imprisonment or deportation of several million people. The word 'repression' (*repressii*), was used in a positive operational sense by Stalin secret police, and it gained wide currency through its use by later Soviet governments (see document 11); but is too vague. Westerners often talk of the 'purges', but the removal and execution of officials was only a part, in time and scale, of the criminal violence of the regime. The term becomes confused, too, with the Communist concept of the bloodless purge or 'cleansing' (*chistka*), the expulsion of unworthy party members. In fact the term 'terror' is the central concept. It communicates the extreme cruelty involved. It unearths historical roots, the Jacobin terror of the 1790s and the Bolshevik 'Red Terror' of 1918. It covers the range of political crimes committed in the Stalin years, which was conceived as terrorism against a range of open and hidden 'class enemies'. Stalinist terror was remarkable in two respects. First of all, the number of its victims was extremely large, and second, among those victims – although by no means making up the the largest share of them – were many high officials. In the first respect the only comparable case in European history was Nazi Germany, in the second Russia was essentially unique.

Peasants and peoples

Collectivisation and its immediate consequences made up the greatest act of terror perpetrated on the Russian population. The economic and social aspects of the Great Breakthrough in the countryside have already been discussed in Chapters 2 and 3. We now have a much better sense of the numerical scale of things, although the official data released since the late 1980s must be assumed still to include great inaccuracies, both intended and unintended. Officially some 381 thousand peasant families (around 1,900 thousand individuals) were deported in 1931 and 1932 as part of collectivisation and dekulakisation. Many of these ended up in what were known as 'special settlements' (*spetsposeleniia*); the number of special settlers reached 1,600 thousand individuals in the middle of 1931 and stayed at the level of about one million throughout the 1930s.[1] This category was later filled out by deported families from among the national minorities (see Chapter 5).

The special settlement was distinct from the better-known corrective labour camps (*ispravitel'no-trudovoi lager'*, ITL). Labour camps had existed since 1918–19, but they took a clearer form during the Great Breakthrough period and were administered from 1934 by a sub-division ('main administration', GU) of the NKVD, the infamous GULAG. The first tidal wave of prisoners into the camps followed on from dekulakisation. There was a net rise in the number of prisoners, from 180 thousand at the start of 1930 to 840 thousand at the start of 1936. Solzhenitsyn' s famous metaphor of the 'GULAG archipelago', the 'islands' of forced labour across the territory of Russia, was an apt one.

Collectivisation also coincided with a lethal wave of executions. Civil executions in the late 1920s and in the 1932–36 period were, according to official figures, in the range of 2,000 to 3,000 a year. In the critical collectivisation years of 1930 and 1931 the numbers were 20,200 and 10,700 respectively. (It was, however, the *indirect* consequences of collectivisation and industrialisation, the estimated 8.5 million 'excess deaths' suffered by the population in 1927–36, that made this the most lethal period of the Stalin years.)

Another broad stream into the GULAG followed from the expansion of the Soviet Union' s borders immediately before and after the Second World War. As we saw in chapter 5, mass arrests and deportations were carried out among the peoples of eastern Poland, the Baltic states and elsewhere. These were followed in wartime by punitive actions against minorities deep within the USSR which were seen as disloyal, the Volga Germans, the Chechen-Ingush, the Crimean Tatars and others. These 'operations' were possible partly because the bureaucracy of terror existed, expanded in 1931–32 and developed even further in 1937–38. Some aspects of this were simply vindictive, such as the fate of some of the Caucasian minorities. Others were 'rational', if despicable; the absorption of border regions was made simpler by eliminating their elites. This aspect of Stalinist terror has parallels with other imperialisms.

A special place in this category of terror against peoples is occupied by one of the most famous crimes of the Stalin years, the execution in cold blood in the spring of 1940 of 15,000 prisoners from the Polish army and the police; the mass grave of a third of these was revealed by the Nazis at Katyn in western Russia 1943 (the two other killing sites were deeper within Russia). This 'operation' involved executions on about the same scale as the official average annual execution toll in the collectivisation years. The executions, which we now know were formally sanctioned at Politburo level, were probably a combination of extreme *deportatsiia* and 1937-style purging of officials. Far from playing a positive role the massacre made it impossible to improve relations with the Polish government in exile, and for fifty years haunted successive Soviet governments.

These two aspects of terror, against the peasants and against some of the minorities, both crimes against humanity, made some 'sense'. Historians may wonder about why the regime decided on rapid comprehensive collectivisation, but once that confrontation had been embarked upon the use of brutal violence was an obvious way of achieving the objective. Stalin was actually probably right about the class struggle intensifying as the country moved closer to socialism, if by this is meant peasant resistance to the regime's attempt to transform their existence from above (see document 3). The resettlement of minority peoples was something found in other countries, and although aspects seem pointless, as well as brutal, the general goal was to secure the boundaries of the enlarged USSR. Both were the product of a political system in which actions could be cloaked in secrecy and implemented by a pre-existing organisation of repression. Much less clear was the 'Great Terror'.

The party and the purges

The most famous aspect of Stalinist terror came two or three years before the Katyn massacre and six or seven years after the worst of the deportations, imprisonment, executions and famine linked to collectivisation. Robert Conquest used the term the 'Great Terror' to describe the events of 1937–38,[2] and this is more accurate than calling them 'the purges' ; the latter term suggesting that repression was confined to members of the Communist party. Although in terms of numbers of victims the Great Terror not the worst of the Stalinist repression, it has attracted the most controversy. For years historians argued about the numbers involved, but we now have more solid information. Much the most striking aspect was the scale of executions which, according to official figures, leapt to 350 thousand in 1937 (fifteen times the previous peak, in 1930) and 330 thousand in 1938. The official size of labour camp population (as distinct from the special settlement population) increased, but not nearly as sharply as the number of executions. The reported numbers only rose from 910 thousand inmates at the start of 1937 (i.e. before the Great Terror) to 1,320 thousand two years later, at the end of 1938. The second striking feature was the identity of many of the victims. The earlier terror involved the deportation, imprisonment and execution of peasants. The later terror struck national minorities. Both groups could conceivably be seen as class or ethnic 'enemies'. Even the Great Terror of 1937–38, it would now seem, was most lethal among those who from their past records or their social origins were regarded as hostile to Soviet power – recidivist criminals, veterans of the civil war White army, former *kulaks*, former members of the middle class. But there was a minority of victims, albeit large in absolute terms, who had been members of the ruling elite. When Khrushchev made his famous 1956 secret speech he focused not on mass victims of terror but on the casualties among the top elite. Communist party congresses assembled the most important party leaders from around the country; the Central Committee elected by a congress was the power elite of the USSR. Of the 1,966 delegates to the 1934 congress, the last before the great terror, no fewer than 1,108 were eventually arrested. Of the national elite, the Central Committee of 139, some 98 – 70 per cent – were reported by Khrushchev as having been arrested and shot.

Historians and politicians have attempted to explain aspects of the events of 1937–38 in quite different ways. For some the Great Terror was part of a calculated campaign for supreme power, motivated by Stalin' s inner cravings. This calculated campaign, it is argued, went back at least to the assassination of Kirov in December 1934. Others see the Great Terror as a logical consequence of Leninism. For a third, revisionist, school the role of accident, institutional confusion, or sinister subordinates is important.

The detailed sequence of events is important in trying to get to grips with the Great Terror of 1937–38. There was, in fact, no obvious concrete causal event, like the collectivisation campaigns of 1930–32, the annexation of the borderlands in 1939–40, or the survival struggle of 1941–45. Stalin's political rivals had been defeated seven years or more earlier, Bukharin, Rykov and Tomskii in 1929–30, Zinoviev, Kamenev and Trotsky in 1927. There had been some mutterings on the fringes of the leadership after the economic disasters of 1930–32 (most famously the Riutin Platform, see document 7), but they had been expeditiously dealt with by the secret police. By the mid-1930s Stalin had no open rival for power, nor was there an obvious challenge from below. In the middle of the 1930s Stalin and his fellow 'victors' should have been basking in the successes of industrialisation and collectivisation in the 'three good years' of 1934, 1935, and 1936.

The assassination of Sergei Kirov in December 1934 is often seen as a critical stage in the birth of the Great Terror. Kirov, head of the Leningrad party organisation, secretary of the Central Committee and member of the Politburo, was shot at party headquarters in Leningrad by a disaffected party member, Leonid Nikolaev. Nikolev was caught at the scene and executed a few days later. Stalin's government was to claim that the assassination was the work of a terrorist conspiracy within the party leadership itself, and this served as a basis for the trials they staged in 1936–38. In contrast many other historians see the terrorist conspiracy against Kirov as being headed by Stalin himself: he arranged the killing either because Kirov was a potential rival for the top leadership or because he was already planning to use the assassination as an excuse to carry out the Great Terror. If Stalin ordered Kirov's killing, using police contacts to expose Kirov to Nikolaev, then he might well have orchestrated the Great Terror. Moreover, if the Soviet leader ordered the assassination of one of his closest colleagues, and a man with whom he evidently had good personal relations, then he was worse even than a vain, suspicious blunderer, he was a quite extraordinary political criminal. On the other hand, if the murder of Kirov was carried out by Nikolaev acting alone, then the 'accidental' side of the Great Terror takes on more substance. Stalin was, at least to some extent, reacting.

The truth probably lies somewhere in between: Nikolaev may have been an independent assassin, but Stalin used the assassination as a pretext to dispose of old and new enemies and to increase his own power. Attempts to prove a link between Stalin and the Kirov assassination have come to nothing, and there have certainly been times – under Khruschev, Gorbachev, and in the post-Soviet era – when it would have been in the interests of the powers that be, who controlled the archives, to prove such an association.[3] It could be argued, too, that however one assesses Stalin's morality, the Kirov assassination was not his 'style'. Stalin was an extraordinary manipulator and intriguer, but he was also cautious, and his actions have to be put in context. It is possible, for example, to know that Stalin and Molotov approved 3,167 death sentences in December 1938, and not accept – without more evidence – that Stalin arranged Kirov's killing four years earlier.

The starting point for the Great Terror was not the assassination of Kirov but the re-arrest of Zinoviev and Kamenev eighteen months later and their public trial in August 1936. Grigorii Zinoviev and Lev Kamenev were veteran leaders of the underground Bolshevik party who had been very close to Lenin. They had held posts at the highest level until they were defeated in the left–right Politburo leadership struggles of the 1920s. They had already been tried once, immediately after the Kirov assassination, when they had been given prison terms for inspiring oppositionists. In the second trial, a year and a half later, the two senior Bolsheviks, and others, confessed in detail to being directly responsible for Kirov's assassination and to belonging to a great anti-Soviet conspiracy. They did this, moreover, in open court and with very wide publicity. It is uncertain how far Stalin believed these confessions, which we now know had been extracted in NKVD torture chambers. But he did in consequence assign a hard-line member of his party apparatus, Nikolai Ezhov, to take over the NKVD. Ezhov enthusiastically pursued charges of conspiracy, and some historians call the whole Great Terror period the *Ezhovshchina* (the 'reign of Ezhov'). A second central 'show trial', of the Old Bolsheviks Georgii Piatakov, Karl Radek and others, was held four months after the first, in January 1937 (see document 10). The process rapidly accelerated after the party Central Committee plenum of February–March 1937. At this meeting the party elite agreed to condemn the 'rightist' leader Bukharin (who supposedly had acted in a bloc with the 'leftists') and accepted the need for both a party purge and mass terror. Party members at lower levels were called upon to denounce traitors, and ripples of condemnation spread throughout the party. By May suspicion fell on the army, and in a large closed trial in June 1937 Marshal Tukhachevskii and a number of other Red Army leaders were condemned and shot.

The terror process in 1937–38 was extraordinarily complex, reaching simultaneously up into the high echelons of the Stalinist leadership and down among former *kulaks*. At the June

1937 plenum of the party Central Committee the first big attacks were launched on senior Stalinists (as opposed to former oppositionists). In the same month emergency three-man tribunals (*troiki*) with powers to make judgements and carry out sentences were put in place in the regions. In July Ezhov set off mass arrests in the provinces. In an order which bore a ghastly resemblance to Stalinist economic planning, regional police leaders were given arbitrary quotas – control figures – to fulfil, so many people to be executed, so many to be exiled. The total 'target' for this 'mass operation' was 73 thousand to execute and 177 thousand to exile. The victims were those who had already been branded anti-Soviet – *kulaks*, for example – common criminals, members of hostile political and nationalist parties and religious activists (see document 11). According to official figures 'only' 1,100 people had been executed in 1936; the 'plan' figure of 73 thousand executions was double the number carried out 1930–31 during the collectivisation crisis, and five times the number of later 'Katyn' victims. This plan was fulfilled, and over-fulfilled, by the police. It was only the beginning of the process; similar orders followed later. From arrests of obvious former enemies the machine turned on Soviet officials.

Revisionist historians, and the Stalinists themselves from later in 1938, argue that local NKVD leaders got out of hand. The second half of 1937 and most of 1938 saw arrests throughout Soviet society: in both the party leadership and rank-and-file, in industry, in the armed forces. The Great Terror continued despite a January 1938 Central Committee condemnation of excesses. There was a third and final show trial in March 1938, this one involving Bukharin, Rykov (Lenin's successor as prime minister) and Iagoda (Ezhov's predecessor in the NKVD). A halt was not implemented until November 1938, when the NKVD was harshly criticised for making groundless arrests, the emergency tribunals that had implemented the mass terror were abolished and Ezhov was dismissed as head of the NKVD. More than one historian has been struck by the similarities between this turnabout and the scaling down of collectivisation in 1930.

Stalin did not oppose the Great Terror of 1937–38, nor was he ignorant of what was going on. The unveiling of enemies was entirely consistent with his class war mentality and his two camp fear of external enemies, indeed of his famous dictum that class conflict intensified the closer the revolution moved to socialism (see document 3). One of the most sensational pieces of evidence that Khrushchev produced in 1956 was Stalin's signing of 300 lists of those to be executed. Stalin almost certainly believed at least some of the charges of conspiracy. He believed, too, that a certain number of innocent people would have to die to be sure of eliminating the 'guilty' ones, and this was a view Molotov, Stalin's chief lieutenant, held forty years later (see document no. 12). It is possible that, like the peasantry in 1930, Russian officialdom proved more cohesive in 1937 than Stalin had expected. The ruling elite of 1937 had, after all, grown into power together from the glory days of the civil war. Some could not believe charges against old comrades. Others, from the police point of view, could not be innocent if their close friends were guilty. Stalin did protect his closest allies in the party leadership, but he felt no particular loyalty to the wider circle of men and women he had appointed to other posts. He may also have felt more comfortable with a new generation who had a Soviet-era education and whose young age and limited personal experience made them ready to accept the Stalinist historical myth without reservations.

What happened – or did not happen – after the Great Terror, from 1939 to 1953, is an important part of the puzzle. We have already seen that repression of the border nationalities intensified. According to newly available official sources the number of executions plummeted to 2,600 in 1939, and 1,600 in 1940. (Some 15,000 Polish POWs were killed in 1940, as well as thousands more from the annexed borderlands, but the official figure – if it is anywhere near accurate – may relate to Soviet citizens only.) The reported annual rate rose again to 8,000 and 23,300 in the first two years of the war and then settled down to between 3,000 and 4,000 in the post-war years. Indeed, the death penalty was abolished in 1947, and only restored in 1950.

In contrast, the labour camp population evidently stayed high through the end of 1941, reaching its peak at the beginning of that year with 1,500 thousand inmates. Some 1,100 thousand inmates were freed in in 1941 and 1942. Even more striking was the number of reported deaths in the chaos and hunger of the early war years: 100 thousand were reported to have died in the GULAG in 1941, 250 thousand in 1942, and 170 thousand in

1943. In contrast the reported toll in the earlier peak year of 1938 had been reported as 'only' 90 thousand. The labour camp population grew steadily from the start of 1944, passing the previous 1941 peak by the start of 1951 (at 1,530 thousand) and ending up at the time of Stalin's death at 1,730 thousand. The population of the labour colonies, used for shorter-term prisoners, was 740 thousand in January 1953; this had peaked in 1949–50 at 1,100 thousand, having grown steadily from 1943. Some of the inmates were accused war criminals and members of the deported national minorities. Others were from among those returned POWs who, after entering 'filtration' camps, were found to have betrayed the motherland. There was an accumulation of prisoners serving long-term sentences. Post-war social turmoil was also an important causal factor: the consequences of natural and state-induced poverty, of enemy occupation and dislocation, and of the difficulties of getting 10 million soldiers back into civilian life. A large share of the prisoners were there for 'pilfering state property', and the GULAG was as much about social control as political terror. It also suited the regime to have a captive labour force for the difficult tasks for post-war reconstruction, vast new public works projects, and especially for the archipelago of nuclear weapons projects. Despite the growing number of prisoners the number of labour camp deaths was evidently much lower than in previous years, although it was still great by absolute standards. Under 20 thousand deaths a year were reported after 1948, which was comparable to the toll in the 'normal' mid-1930s but with a camp population that was now twice the size.

This later period of Stalinist terror is normally identified with Lavrentii Beria, who replaced Ezhov as NKVD head in late 1938. Beria eventually became a scapegoat, like Ezhov, but of rather a different type. He was purged by the new leadership in 1953 – indeed he was the last really high-level 'victim' of state terror in the history of the USSR, executed 38 years before the system finally collapsed. Khrushchev made Beria an arch-villain in the 1956 secret speech and in his taped memoirs. The real picture is rather more complicated, not least because Khrushchev tried to hide his own considerable guilt. Beria was in fact an extraordinary political maneuverer, a man who unsuccessfully played the liberal card in 1953, three years before Khrushchev. Beria implemented the halting of the Great Terror in the winter of 1938–39, although a number of imprisoned senior Communists would be executed after that date. He also only had direct control of the whole secret police for less than half the post-1937 period. The NKVD was divided into two commissariats in 1941, and again in 1943 (the NKVD and the NKGB, the Commissariat of Internal Affairs and the Commissariat of State Security; the people's commissariats became ministries in 1946, and these two commissariats became the MVD and the MGB). Beria was not even head of the MVD after March 1946, although he took it over again for a few months after Stalin' s death. During these years Stalin evidently played one police organisation off again the others. A key figure was V. S. Abakumov, who was head of *Smersh* (the wartime military counter-intelligence organisation) from 1943, and of the MGB from 1946 until his arrest in 1951. Late in his life Stalin made use of M. D. Riumin, Abakumov's former deputy and head of the MGB' s investigation department, but nevertheless Beria carried a great deal of weight with Stalin as a deputy prime minister, and the wartime deportations were his responsibility.

The security organs exercised a high degree of 'vigilance' after 1945, and were used with effect for social control and against national minorities. The political elite were, however, much more secure. There were secret trials in the air force and navy, about which much more is now known, but the number of victims were small compared to 1937–38, and they can probably be explained by the desire on the secret police to show vigilance. Marshal Zhukov, whom most sources would see as the embodiment of the interests of the Red Army, was posted to provincial commands, but he was not directly persecuted. The so-called Leningrad Affair of 1949–50 is often seen as the result not solely of Stalin's abuse of power but of competition between rival cliques, followers of Politburo members Zhdanov and Malenkov. A number of officials who had come out of Zhdanov's Leningrad organisation won posts of national importance after 1946. Two of these were A. A. Kuznetsov, a party Central Committee secretary, and N. A. Voznesenskii, co-ordinator of the wartime economy and head of the State Planning Committee (*Gosplan*); both were Politburo members. Kuznetsov was arrested, with others, in August 1949 and Voznesenskii in October 1949, the first

Politburo-level arrests since 1938. If Stalin was responsible and trying to make some kind of point, it was revealed very slowly. Zhdanov, the erstwhile patron of the Leningraders, had died of natural causes over a year before the arrests. A year would pass between the arrests and the trial and execution (in October 1950) and, unlike the events of 1937–38, everything took place in secrecy. The fall of MVD head Abakumov in July 1951 might be placed in the same category of political terror, although Abakumov was not a Politburo member, and he was executed not by Stalin, but in late 1954 by Stalin's successors.

The final episode in the history of Stalinist terror is the so-called 'Doctors' Plot'. It seems fitting that Stalin's career, which contained so many mysteries and controversies, should have ended with such an enigma. Stalin died on 5 March 1953; two months earlier, on 13 January, *Pravda* announced the arrest of a number of Kremlin doctors, most of them Jews. They were accused of having had poisoned Soviet leaders. Some historians speculate that the Doctors' Plot might have developed, had Stalin not died, into another Great Terror. It is not clear whether this was Stalin's masterpiece or a product of a perverse culture of 'vigilance' in which power-seeking elements in the police (Riumin) played on the ageing dictator' s suspicions. Beria was blamed, but it is now clear that he (like Iagoda in 1936) was himself under attack for showing insufficient vigilance. Certainly some older members of Stalin' s Politburo – Molotov, Mikoian, Voroshilov – were out of favour. Nevertheless there is substantial evidence that in the course of 1951–52 the septuagenarian dictator' s ability to influence events was on the wane.[4] Some credence can be given to the suggestion that his subordinates either hastened his death or did little to deal with an actual stroke; perhaps the decapitation of the elite was only possible once.

******

We now know that the numbers involved in the terror fluctuated over time, and were less than some of the extreme high estimates. At least there is no school of denial as in the case of the Nazi holocaust. There were mass executions, of which Katyn is the most famous, and even isolated cases of lethal medical experiments on humans, but the NKVD did not have extermination camps which industrialised death, nor did it carry out anything comparable to the mass shooting of Jews by the SS murder detachments in Eastern Europe and Russia. But the Stalinist record is truly appalling, and it is irrelevant that the Nazis were even worse.

Terror, directed outwards and upwards, was a defining feature of the Stalinist dictatorship. Other periods of Soviet history featured wide-scale persecution of political opponents. In the civil war of 1917–20 terror was enthusiastically adopted. Under Stalin, however, the number of victims was incomparably higher, and it was only then that terror was turned on the regime's own leadership. The Soviet system was unpleasant after Stalin's death, but it would never apply terror on such a scale and in such directions again. The institutions of terror, the secret police and the camp system, were most fully developed in his time. From this it might be possible to reach the conclusion that such terror was the product of a unique, powerful and deranged, mind. That would, however, oversimplify a complex situation.

Stalin did what he did not because he was betraying the revolution, but because he was faithfully carrying it out. Terror had its roots in the revolutionary tradition and in a view of the world held by a generation of leaders. Intolerant politics were inherent in Bolshevism. Lenin's seminal *What is to be Done?* of 1902 had on its cover a quotation from a letter from Lassalle to Marx, with the passage: 'the party will consolidate itself to the extent that it purges itself'. Stalin himself would repeat this in 1924: 'The party becomes strong by purging itself of opportunist elements' – not by arguing with them within the party.[5] It was a double point, first ideological purity and second its achievement not by argument but by expulsion. The civil war enhanced a belief in a life-or-death political struggle; it led to a rejection of legal limitations on state power, to an acceptance of terror and to the institutionalisation of a powerful political police. Enthusiasm for the programme of the rapid transformation of a traditional society was not confined to Stalin, and from hindsight the conflict with the peasants was almost inevitably bound to lead to massive casualties. As we know, it led, directly and indirectly, to the death or exile of millions of people. The secondary result of the conflict of the early 1930s was the expansion of the police and prison camp system and a confirmation of the psychology of struggle. But the pitched battle ended not in 1953 but twenty years earlier. It was not repeated because the Great Breakthrough had been achieved. It is true that from pitched battle the regime settled down to a long grinding process of attrition, one symptom of which was the high GULAG population throughout the late 1940s. Nevertheless the process of pacification was different from that of conquest.

To jump forward in time, the terror directed against the nationalities – especially the mass deportations – had features in common with collectivisation. Although it can be divided into two or three deportation campaigns, before, during, and after the Second World War, it was a finite event. Once the minority borderlands had been incorporated or re-incorporated into the Soviet motherland, once the glacis of satellite states had been established, extreme measures ceased to be necessary. There was to be a continuing process of pacification, in this case including counter-insurgency campaigns in the western borderlands, but the rate of deportations declined after the early post-war years.

So the battles for economic transformation and the integration of the border nationalities had their own logical ends; they did not end because of Stalin's death in 1953, and they were scaling down before he died. The more complex, if less lethal, political confrontation of the regime with its own people also changed over time. Involved here were both the integrity of the internal political system and the weight of the external and internal perceived threat. The 1930s were unique in the Russian experience for two reasons, both connected with the insecurity of the Soviet regime.

On the one hand Nazi Germany and Imperial Japan did in that decade represent an extraordinary and unique danger to Soviet Russia (and the international status quo in general), because of their militarism and ultra-nationalist aggressive policies. Russia was especially threatened because of its diplomatic isolation and economic weakness. In the early NEP period, in contrast, an immediate generalised threat from 'imperialism' was probably not taken very seriously by the top leadership. And by the 1950s the USSR held a position of strength, with powerful and successful conventional forces, significant allies in Eastern Europe and east Asia, and nuclear deterrent forces. So the external threat was unusually strong in the 1930s, compared to other decades.

On the other hand in the 1930s the administrative system and the armed forces of the USSR was still in transition. They were more consolidated than they had been in the 1920s, but they were untested. Both the political and technical elite had grown up in Tsarist Russia. The Communist party comprised only a small proportion of the population. Bitter factional fighting within the elite was a very recent memory. The situation was different in the 1950s and 1960s, not only because Stalin was dead, but because the 'threat' was different. The external enemies were weaker, more distant, or less aggressive; the internal system was more consolidated, much more sure of itself.

Late Stalinist, post-war, Russia was deeply oppressive, more oppressive than other states, but *mass* terror was not then an essential part of the system. Campaigns of physical terror directed against large numbers of the ethnic Russian population, campaigns of physical terror directed against the elite, ceased. The 1945–53 period was in some respects more like the beginning of Khrushchev's 1950s than the end of Ezhov's 1930s. As far as this aspect of terror was concerned, lessons had been learned, probably by Stalin and certainly by the elite around him. Terrorism turned out to be hard to control, and it could be counter-productive. The elite of 1937 had gone to their deaths partly because they did not expect a lethal purge to be directed against them. The elite that replaced them would not be so naive. Terror was in abeyance after 1953, not only because the architect of terror was dead, but because terror had achieved its objectives. More important, victory 'proved' the material strength of the system and brought in Russian nationalism as a sturdy prop of the system. The post-Great Terror elite had eventually proved itself in the war. The accelerated promotion of a generation of Soviet-educated leaders, managers and commanders may have reduced Stalin' s suspicions. Stalin sid not embark on general terror against Slavic officials or civilians in the last fifteen years of his life, and neither would his successors.

By far the most numerous victims of Stalinist terror were the peasants, not the party elite. Just because oppression of peasants is more comprehensible than the self-destruction of the Soviet elite that does not mean it was less important. Terror, in its different guises, was not an accidental part of the Soviet system, but neither was it necessarily a permanent feature. It may have been an unavoidable part of Soviet evolution, what Lenin called in another context a 'disease of childhood'. The terroristic system as it actually evolved in the Stalin years may well have been inconceivable without the particular personality of Joseph Stalin, without the fact that it was being put into practice for the first time, but it was also inconceivable without the legacy of Bolshevism and without the world situation as it was in the 1930s and 1940s.

Notes

1 Most of the figures given in this chapter for the number of victims come from two recent archive-based articles: J. A. Getty *et al.*, 'Victims of the Soviet penal system in the post-war years', *American Historical Review*, 98:4 (1993), 1017–49, and S. Wheatcroft, 'The scale of German and Soviet repression and mass killings, 1930–45', *Europe–Asia Studies*, 48:8 (1996) 1319–55.

2 R. Conquest, *The Great Terror: A Reassessment* (Oxford, 1990). For Conquest as the origin of the term see K. Dushenko, *Russkie politicheskie tsitaty: Ot Lenina do El' tsina* [*Russian Political quotations from Lenin to Stalin*] (Moscow, 1996), p. 166. The term 'Great Terror' also presumably owes something to the French *Grande Peur* (Great Fear) of 1789, although that was essentially the action of peasants against landlords. Another historian has coined an apt term, the 'Lesser Terror', to describe the events of 1939–53: M. Parrish *The Lessor Terror: Soviet State Security 1930–1953* (Westport CO, 1996).

3 Classic presentation of the Stalin conspiracy interpretation include R. Tucker, *Stalin in Power 1928–1941* (New York, 1990), pp. 274–6, 288–96, and R. Conquest, *Stalin and the Kirov Assassination* (New York, 1989). Recent revisionist accounts are Getty, in A. Getty and R.T. Manning (eds), *Stalinist Terror: New Perspectives* (Cambridge, 1993), pp. 42–9, and R. Thurston, *Life and Terror in Stalin's Russia 1934–1941* (New Haven CT, 1996), pp. 20–2. For a discussion of the most recent findings using new Russian material see R. W. Davies, *Soviet History in the Yeltsin Era* (Basingstoke, 1997), pp. 156–8.

4 See Chapter 1, note 3.

5 Stalin, 'Ob osnovakh leninizma' ['Foundations of Leninism'], *Sochineniia*, vol. 6, pp. 183–6.

Conclusion

Through storms the sun of freedom shone for us,
And the great Lenin lit our way.
Stalin brought us up to be true to the people,
And inspired us to labour and heroic deeds.

Soviet national anthem, 1944

'They say that victors may not be judged, that they should not be criticised or checked up on. This is wrong. Victors may and must be judged, they may and must be criticised and checked up on.'[1] Stalin's speech to his Moscow electors in February 1946, in the wake of the great victory, needs to be taken even more seriously than he intended. The tone of the speech was one of self-congratulation, for the Great Breakthrough of industrialisation and collectivisation and for victory over Nazi Germany. There would indeed be further achievements before the end of the Stalin years – economic reconstruction, creation of a vast socialist bloc, the status of a nuclear power. The paradox is the combination of awesome achievement – industrialisation, military victory, internal and international power – and awesome failings.

Russian historians were from the late 1980s able to begin filling in what Gorbachev called the 'blank spots' of their country's history. The interpretations published in Russia are fundamentally different from the official view of the 1970s and 1980s, and of the Khrushchev era. They document the cruelties and failings of even the early Stalin years and go back to challenge the achievements of the revolution. Does this mean, however, that there

113

should be a change in the way that *western* historians look at Stalinism?

Despite the new perspectives, Iosif Vissarionovich Dzhugashvili-Stalin was still a cause of Stalinism. Of the little clique pool of leaders around Lenin in 1921 it is hard to see another who would have acted as Stalin did. What is clearer from the new sources is Stalin's individual contribution to radical policies – forced collectivisation, increasing the pace of industrialisation, exaggerating the climate of vigilance and personally supervising the high-level purge, confronting the west. This is not to say, counter-factually, that the Communist party without Stalin would not have repressed the population, minorities and Russians alike, developed a military-industrial complex, or operated within a system of confrontation with its enemies. Much of that continued after Stalin's death. However, the years after Stalin are particularly important for understanding what happened before his death in 1953. The *excesses* of Stalinism had much to do with Stalin himself, and were not an essential part of the Soviet system. The 'permanent purge' was in fact an impermanent product of Stalin's own lifetime, later economic policies were much more cautious, and the international confrontation was more sensibly managed. And taking this 'intentionalist' view a step further, it is important to stress just how negatively Stalin must be assessed. He was not simply cruel, he also caused Russia and the Russian people enormous harm. Despite being intelligent, cunning and hard working, he was also vastly incompetent.

On the other hand the Stalin years were to an extent the logical consequence of 1917. Even in Soviet Russia the perceived starting point of Stalin's mistakes moved back from 1937 (under Khrushchev) to 1929 (under Gorbachev), and the official interpretation could not have gone any further back without the regime denying itself. Stalin saw himself as the continuer, the personification, of the revolution, and that self-perception was not inaccurate; to a large extent his goals were ones which the makers of the revolution would have shared. Stalinism is incomprehensible without its Marxist-Leninist emphasis on class conflict, and this represents a continuity going back to the foundation of the movement. It determined both internal priorities and the impossibility of normal relations with the outside world

– the two camps. Likewise the Marxist rejection of the market, which dated back to 1917, pre-determined the nature of the economic system. Much of what happened under Stalin can be explained by the grotesque mismatch between the ideology of industrial socialism and the realities of peasant Russia; that mismatch was there also in the time of the underground Bolshevik party. At the same time Stalin's goals may even have been a logical continuation of the nation-building, modernising, objectives of pre-revolutionary Russian statesmen, where there was a similar mismatch between international aspirations and a backward society.

What was the character of the system? The concept of totalitarianism is alive and well, partly thanks to the politicians, journalists and historians of the new Russia who have embraced *totalitarizm*. Of course the more we know from the documents about the rickety nature of the Stalinist system the less convincing is the idea of a Orwellian 'total' totalitarianism, with absolute power in the hands of an all-powerful dictator. The great contribution of the social historians has been to show the dynamic rather than the static nature of the system, Big Brother trying to operate in a 'quicksand society'. However, Stalinism (like Nazism) was the product of its time. Definitions of totalitarianism – in Russia, Germany, or Italy – need to take into account the fact that it was an *historical* concept. It was not just an abstract series of characteristics or symptoms, but a result of a particular stage of historical development. The key features of this were the failure of existing (monarchical/autocratic) political-social systems, in an era of highly-charged international tension, and with the availability of new technologies for communication, mass mobilisation and mass destruction.

Looking at Stalinism from the late 1990s, we have a different perspective from that of observers in the 1950s or the 1960s, or even in the 1970s and 1980s. With the post-Cold War collapse of the Marxist Left, the issue of Stalinism is no longer of political importance; Stalin is even more an historical figure. Stalin's legacy is also now even more flawed than it seemed to earlier generations. We now know that the suffering of the Stalin years did not even have a positive 'historical role'. It did not create something permanent – a powerful socialist economic system, a robust polity or a sphere of influence at least over central Europe.

115

It did not create an enduring culture or even, at an individual level, the 'new Soviet person'. Perhaps most strikingly, and to the surprise of western experts and Soviet leaders alike, it did not overwhelm a sense of ethnic nationalism among the minorities.

We have now also to see Stalin's influence on the collapse of the Soviet system, to consider the continuities across nearly four decades between Stalin's death and the death of the system itself in 1991. This was a form of continuity that was not considered in earlier debates. On the one hand many of the institutions and programmes of the Stalin years survived him, the *nomenklatura* bureaucracy, the top-heavy planning system with its focus on the military industrial complex, the unholy mix of socialism and Russian chauvinism. They turned out to be unreformable, and in the end they prevented the successful continuation or adaptation of the system, at least in its entirety. Features of Stalinism endured partly because Stalin had mixed success and failure, creating at great cost a powerful heavy industry and preserving at even greater cost national independence. They endured also because they confirmed the position of the ruling bureaucracy which Stalin had put in place both institutionally and individually. On the other hand the Stalinist programme was corrosive to the system in another, more positive sense. Lenin and Stalin saw capitalism and imperialism as doomed by their own internal contradictions, but the same could be said of Stalinism and Soviet Russia. In the long term the Great Breakthrough of economic and social change created a complex, urbanised, educated, society that was incompatible with the watered-down Leninist-Stalinist poitical system which survived to the 1980s; this was true both for the ethnic Russians and for the minorities. The Stalin years were, in the end, pivotal to Russian history, but not in a way that Stalin himself had intended.

Note

1   Stalin, *Sochineniia*, vol. 3[16], p. 20. Laughter and cheers accompanied this part of the speech.

Selected documents

Note: Ellipses ([…]) between paragraphs denote at least one paragraph of the original text having been left out.

Document 1

Socialism in one country

This excerpt comes from the preface to a collection of Stalin's articles and was entitled 'The October Revolution and the tactics of the Russian Communists'. It was written in December 1924, eleven months after Lenin's death, and was part of the so-called 'literary debate' within the party leadership. It was one of the first uses of the doctrine of 'socialism in one country' which, advocated by Stalin and his erstwhile Politburo ally, Bukharin, was to become the party's policy at the 14th party congress in December 1925. Stalin set himself in opposition to a doctrine of 'permanent revolution', which he based on a quotation from Trotsky's 1922 book, *The Year 1905*: 'The contradictions in the position of a workers' government in a backward country in which the peasant population are the overwhelming majority can be solved only on an international scale, in the arena of the world proletarian revolution'.

From: I. V. Stalin, *Voprosy leninizma*, 11th ed. (Moscow, 1945), pp. 90f, 102, 104.

[Trotsky says that] since there is still no victory in the West, the only 'choice' that remains for the revolution in Russia is: either to

117

rot away or to degenerate into a bourgeois state.

[...]

Lenin's theory of the proletarian revolution is the repudiation of the theory of 'permanent revolution'.

Lack of faith in the strength and abilities of our revolution, lack of faith in the strength and abilities of the Russian proletariat – that is the root of the theory of the 'permanent revolution'.

[...]

What distinguishes Trotsky's theory from the ordinary Menshevik theory that the victory of socialism in one country, and in a backward country at that, is impossible without the preliminary victory of the proletarian revolution 'in the principal countries of Western Europe'? [The Mensheviks were the moderate wing of Russian Marxism, and opposed the 1917 seizure of power by the radical wing, the Bolsheviks. Trotsky had been an independent Menshevik until 1917, and his Old Bolshevik political opponents used this against him.]

In essence there is no difference.

[...]

There can be no doubt that the universal theory of a simultaneous victory of the revolution in the principal countries of Europe, the theory that the victory of the socialism in one country is impossible [i.e. Trotsky's 'permanent revolution'], has proved to be an artificial and unviable theory. The seven years' history of the proletarian revolution in Russia speaks not for but against this theory. This theory is unacceptable not only as a scheme of development in the world revolution, for which it contradicts obvious facts. It is still less acceptable as a slogan, for it fetters, rather than releases, the initiative of individual countries which have the possibility, by reason of well-known historical conditions, to break through the front of capital independently; for it stimulates not an active onslaught on capital in individual counties, but a passive waiting for the moment of the 'universal denouement' [...] Lenin was absolutely right in saying that the victory of the proletariat in one country is the 'typical case', that a simultaneous revolution in a number of countries' can only be a 'rare exception'. [Here and below Stalin cites Lenin's *Works*.]

[...]

While it is true that the *final* victory of socialism in the first country to free itself is impossible without the combined efforts of the proletarians of several countries, it is equally true that the unfolding of the world revolution will be the more rapid and thorough, the more effective the assistance rendered by the first socialist country to the workers and labouring masses in all other countries.

In what way should this assistance be expressed?

It should be expressed, firstly, in the victorious country 'achieving the utmost possible in one country for the development, support and awakening of the revolution *in all countries'*.

It should be expressed, secondly, in that the 'victorious proletariat' of one country, 'having expropriated the capitalists and organised for itself social production, would stand up ... *against* the rest of the world, the capitalist world, attracting to itself the oppressed classes of the other countries, raising revolts in those countries against the capitalists, and acting if necessary even with military forces against the exploiting classes and their states.

The characteristic feature of this assistance given by the victorious country is not only that it hastens the victory of the proletarians of other countries, but also that, by facilitating this victory, it ensures the *final* victory of socialism in the first victorious country.

Document 2

There are no fortresses ...

This is an excerpt from a long speech by Stalin in April 1928 to a meeting of Moscow party activists, at the start of what has been called the 'cultural revolution'. The military metaphor, harking back to the civil war, is typical of Stalinist discourse.

From: I. V. Stalin, *Sochineniia* [*Works*], vol. 11 (Moscow, 1954), pp. 57–9.

They say that it is impossible for Communists, and especially Communist economic-managers who come from the working class, to master chemical formulas or technical knowledge in general. That is not true, comrades. There are in the world no fortresses the working people, the Bolsheviks, cannot storm. (*Applause.*) We captured tougher fortresses than these during our struggle against the bourgeoisie. Everything depends on the desire to master technical knowledge and on arming ourselves with persistence and Bolshevik patience. But in order to alter the condition of work of our economic cadres and to help them become real and fully-fledged masters of their jobs, we must abolish the old model regulations and replace them with new ones. Otherwise we run the risk of maiming our own people. [The 'model regulations' conferred power on the 'technical director', typically a specialist trained in Tsarist days, over the 'general director' appointed by the Communists.]

Document 3

The sharpening of the class struggle

Stalin's first formulation of the concept of the sharpening of the class struggle came in a long speech to a Central Committee plenum in July 1928. All of this was symptomatic of his growing distance from the more moderate 'rightist' Bukharin. Stalin later used this concept to justify the purges.

From: Stalin, *Sochineniia*, vol. 11, pp. 171f.

[T]he more we advance, the greater will be the resistance of the capitalist elements and the sharper will be the class struggle [...] It must not be imagined that the socialist forms [of the economy] will develop, squeezing out the enemies of the working class, while our enemies retreat in silence and make way for our advance, that then we shall again advance and they will again retreat until 'unexpectedly' all the social groups without exception, both kulaks and poor peasants, both workers and capitalists, find themselves 'suddenly', 'imperceptibly', without struggle or commotion, in the lap of a socialist society. In general such fairy-tales do not happen and especially not in the conditions of the dictatorship of the proletariat.

It never has been and never will be the case that a dying class surrenders its positions voluntarily without attempting to organise resistance. It never has been and never will be the case that the working class could advance toward socialism in a class society without struggle or commotion. On the contrary, the advance toward socialism cannot but cause the exploiting elements to resist the advance, and the resistance of the exploiters cannot but lead to the inevitable sharpening of the class struggle.

That is why the working class must not be lulled with talk about the class struggle playing a secondary role.

Document 4

The Great Breakthrough

The excerpt below come from an article Stalin published in *Pravda* on the occasion of the twelfth anniversary of the Bolshevik revolution on 7 November 1929. The article not only signalled the start of general, forced collectivisation of agriculture but marked the effective end of the New Economic Policy of 1921. This language, especially the military metaphors ('front', 'offensive'), is typical of the time. The Russian word *perelom* is difficult to translate, but it is not itself a military term; 'breakthrough', however, conveys Stalin's sense of the word better than 'great change' or 'turning point', which are other translations. Timasheff's influential concept of the 'great retreat' derives from Stalin's 'great breakthrough'.

From: Stalin, *Voprosy leninizma*, pp. 264–6, 268, 274.

The past year was a year of a great breakthrough [*velikii perelom*] on all fronts of socialist construction. The keynote of this breakthrough has been, and continues to be, a decisive *offensive* of socialism against capitalist elements in town and country. [...]

[O]ur party succeeded in making good use of our retreat during the first stages of the NEP [New Economic Policy] in order, in the later stages, to organise the *breakthrough* and the launch a *successful offensive* against the capitalist elements.

[...]

[O]ne of the most important facts, if not the most important fact, of our work of construction during the past year is that we have succeeded in bringing about a *decisive breakthrough* in the sphere of productivity of labour. This breakthrough has found expression in a growth of the *creative initiative* and powerful *labour enthusiasm* of millions of members of the working class on the front of socialist construction. This is our first and fundamental *achievement* during the past year.

[...]

Inseparably connected with the first achievement of the party is its second achievement. This [...] consists of the fact that during the past year we have in the main successfully solved the *problem of accumulation* for capital construction in heavy industry, we have achieved an *accelerated tempo* in the development of the production of the means of production and have created the preconditions for transforming our country into a country of *metal*.

[...]

Finally, about the party's third achievement during the past year, an achievement organically connected with the two previous achievements. I am referring to the *fundamental breakthrough* in the development of our agriculture from small-scale and backward *individual* farming to large-scale, advanced, *collective* agriculture, to joint cultivation of land, to machine-tractor stations, to artels [a form of agricultural co-operation] and collective farms [*kolkhozy*], based on modern technology, and, finally, to giant state farms [*sovkhozy*], equipped with hundreds of tractors and harvester combines.

[...]

We are moving at full steam ahead along the track of industrialisation – to socialism, leaving behind our age-old 'Russian' [*rasseiskaia*] backwardness. We are becoming a country of metal, a country of automobiles, a country of tractors. And when we have put the USSR on an automobile, and the peasant [*muzhik*] on a tractor, let the worthy capitalists, who boast so much of their 'civilisation', try to catch us up! We shall see which countries may then be 'classified' as backward, and which as advanced.

Document 5

Dizzy with success

The following are excerpts from an article published by Stalin in *Pravda* in March 1930, in the aftermath of the previous winter's forced collectivisation.

From: Stalin, *Voprosy leninizma*, pp. 300, 303f.

The successes of our collective-farm policy are explained, among other things, by the fact that it rests on the *voluntary character* of the collective-farm movement and on *taking into account the diversity of conditions* in the various regions of the USSR. Collective farms must not be established by force. That would be foolish and reactionary. The collective-farm movement must rest on the active support of the main mass of the peasantry.

[...]

We know that in a number of regions of the USSR [...] attempts are being made to skip the artel framework and to leap straight into the agricultural commune. [Artels were a looser form of collective farm, based on the peasants keeping their private plots and some of their livestock.]

[...]

How could there have arisen in our midst such block-headed exercises in 'socialisation', such ludicrous attempts to overleap oneself, attempts which aim at by-passing classes and the class struggle, and which in fact bring grist to the mill of our class enemies? They could have arisen only in the atmosphere of our 'easy' and 'unexpected' successes on the front of collective-farm development. They could have arisen only as a result of the block-headed mood among a section of our party: 'We can achieve anything!'. 'There's nothing we cannot do!' They could have arisen only because some of our comrades have become dizzy with success and for the moment have lost clearness of mind and sobriety of vision.

[...]

One must not lag behind the movement, because to do so is to lose contact with the masses. But neither must one run too far ahead, because to run too far ahead is to lose connection with the masses.

Document 6

Those who fall behind get beaten

The following extract comes from one of Stalin's most quoted speeches, delivered to a conference of Soviet economic mangers on 4 February 1931. It is important for the link between economic tempo, a new Russian nationalism ('the socialist fatherland'), and a world in struggle.

From: Stalin, *Voprosy leninizma*, pp. 328f.

It is sometimes asked if it is not possible to slow the tempo somewhat, to hold back. No, comrades, it is not possible! It is not possible to reduce the tempo! On the contrary we must increase it as much as we can with all our powers and possibilities. This is demanded of us by our obligations to the workers and peasants of the USSR. This is demanded of us by our obligations to the working class of the whole world.

To reduce the tempo means to fall behind. Those who fall behind get beaten. But we do not want to be the ones who are beaten. No, we do not want that! One feature of the history of Russia was continuous beatings for backwardness. She was beaten by the Mongol khans. She was beaten by the Turkish beys. She was beaten by the Swedish feudal lords. She was beaten by the Polish-Lithuanian gentry. She was beaten by the Anglo-French capitalists. She was beaten by the Japanese barons. She was beaten by all of them – for her backwardness. For the backwardness of her military, for the backwardness of her culture, for the backwardness of her state, for the backwardness of her industry, for the backwardness of her agriculture. [...]

[...]

In the past we did not have and could not have a fatherland [*otechestvo*]. But now, when we have overthrown capitalism, and we have workers in power – we have a fatherland, and we will maintain its independence. [...]

We are fifty to a hundred years behind the advanced countries. We must make up this distance in ten years. Either we do it, or we shall go under.

That is what is dictated to us by our obligations before the workers and peasants of the USSR.

But we have another, more serious and more important, obligation. That is a obligation before the world proletariat. [...] We must move forward so that the working class of the whole world, watching us, can say: there it is, my advanced detachment, there it is, my shock brigade, there it is, my workers' power, there it is, my fatherland – they are fulfilling their cause, our cause – well – we will support them against the capitalists and will ignite the cause of the world revolution.

Document 7

The Riutin platform

The full title of this platform was 'Stalin and the Crisis of the Proletarian Dictatorship'. The author, M. N. Riutin (1890–1937), was a worker of peasant origins who had joined the Bolshevik party in 1914. Riutin became a senior leader in the late 1920s, party secretary of one of the most important industrial boroughs of Moscow, and a member of the Central Committee, but he was excluded from the party in 1930 after a denunciation. The platform was first drafted in March 1932 and was approved by a secret meeting in Moscow in August of Riutin's tiny 'Union of Marxist-Leninists' . The group was arrested, and Riutin himself was shot at the start of the purges. The platform was not published until 1990, and even then it was based on a typed version compiled by the secret police. There are possible doubts about the correctness of the text. Nevertheless the 1932 platform of the Union was indirectly one of the most influential documents of the Stalin period. Senior party leaders who read copies of the original were later purged for not having reported it to the authorities, and Stalin may well have seen it as symptomatic of 'wavering' among senior leaders. The excerpts below are just the conclusion of a much longer survey of the Stalin period; the police typescript was 194 pages long.

From: *Izvestiia Tsentral'nogo komiteta*, 1990, no. 12, pp. 197–9.

In the struggle with Stalin and his clique it is necessary to avoid one very widely held illusion, that this struggle can be begun and can be led by the former Trotskyist leaders who have repented or by the former leaders of the 'right opposition'.

This would be the deepest mistake. The majority of them now are a spent force for the struggle with Stalin.

They hate Stalin with all the fibres of their souls [...]

But for now they will either be silent, sitting it out and waiting, and some of them will even lower themselves to fawn before Stalin.

For the struggle to destroy the dictatorship of Stalin it is necessary to count for the most part not on old leaders, but on new forces [...]

The struggle will give birth to leaders and heroes.

It is necessary to begin to act. This struggle will demand sacrifices. [...]

[...]

In concrete terms, the range of measures necessary to get the party and the country out of the crisis and dead end, are essentially the following:

I.   In the area of the party.

    1. Liquidation of the dictatorship of Stalin and his clique.

    2. Immediate replacement of all heads of the party apparatus and the calling of new elections to party organs on the basis of genuine intra-party democracy and with the creation of firm organisational guarantees against the usurpation of party rights by the party apparatus.

                   [...]

II. In the area of the soviets [i.e. the state]

                   [...]

    3. Renewal and decisive purge of the apparatus of the GPU [secret police].

III. In the area of industrialisation.

    1. An immediate end to the anti-Leninist methods of industrialisation and an irresponsible tempo leading to the exploitation of the working class, the employees and the countryside [and] leading to direct and indirect, open and hidden, unbearable taxes and inflation. Industrialisation to be carried out on the basis of the real and unwavering growth of the well-being of the masses.

                   [...]

IV. In the area of agriculture

    1. Immediate disbanding of all collective farms which are created by force and are a sham. Real voluntary collectivisation on the basis of machine technology and all possible help to the collective farms.

    2. Immediate creation of concrete measures to develop individual peasant undertakings by poor and middle peasants.

                   [...]

    6. Immediate cessation of requisitioning of grain, livestock, and other produce by the current method of looting the countryside.

                   [...]

V.   In the area of trade.

    1. Ending the export of agriculture produce at negligible prices.

[...]

VI. In the area of finance and fiscal matters.

   1. Ending inflation, which is falling as a heavy tax borne by the proletariat and all working people.

[...]

VII In the area of the material and legal conditions of the mass of workers and peasants.

[...]

   2. Restoration of the old regulations for workers leaving enterprises, which existed four years ago. [Labour movement had become more restricted in the intervening period.]

   3. Restoration of the old laws and of Leninist policy in the work of the trade unions.

   4. To end immediately the adventurist policy of dekulakisation in the countryside, which in fact in directed against all inhabitants of the countryside.

Document 8

Engineers of human souls

This excerpt is from a recently-published transcript of Stalin's comments at an informal meeting with forty-five members of the literary intelligentsia. This took place at the Moscow villa of the well-known writer Maksim Gor'kii on 26 October 1932. Stalin's colleagues Molotov, Voroshilov and Kaganovich also attended.

From: A. Kemp-Welch, *Stalin and the Literary Intelligentsia* (London, 1991), pp. 128–31.

What is the essence of today's meeting? Its essence lies in the relationship between party and non-party writers. [...] Lenin always said that the nub of the problem is that the party must always carry non-party people with it. [...] The party is small, but non-party people are numerous. [...]

Why did we liquidate RAPP? [The Russian Association of Proletarian Writers was abolished in May 1932.] Because RAPP was cut off from non-party writers, because it ceased serious party work in literature. [...] Sectarianism created an unhealthy atmosphere, not conducive to trust. We disbanded all groups and removed the biggest group – RAPP – which was responsible for sectarianism. [...]

How will we organise the Writers' Union? In the centre will be a strong nucleus and around them a wide strata of non-party writers.

[...]

I forgot to talk about what you are 'producing'. There are various forms of production: artillery, automobiles, lorries. You also produce 'commodities', 'works', 'products'. Such things are highly necessary. Engineering things. For people's souls. 'Products' are highly necessary too. 'Products' are very important for people's souls. You are engineers of human souls. Your work is in vain if the souls in them are rotten. No, 'production' of souls is a most important task.

The whole production of the country is linked to your 'production'. And that, in its turn, is not entrusted without the understanding that people enter life when they take part in the production of socialism. As someone here rightly said, the writer cannot sit still, he must get to know the life of the country. Rightly said. Men are transforming life. That is why I propose a toast 'To Engineers of Human Souls'.

Document 9

Socialist realism

The doctrine of 'socialist realism' was laid down by the party's leading ideologist, Andrei Zhdanov, in his opening address to the first congress of the Writers Union in August 1934. This remained the official doctrine of the creative intelligentsia until the end of the Soviet period.

From: A. A. Zhdanov, *On Literature, Music and Philosophy* (London, 1950), pp. 13, 16–17.

The present position of bourgeois literature is such that it is already incapable of producing great works. *The decline and decay of bourgeois literature derive from the decline and decay of the capitalist system and are a feature and aspect characteristic of the present condition of bourgeois culture and literature.*

[...]

A riot of mysticism, religious mania and pornography is characteristic of the decline and decay of bourgeois culture. The 'celebri-
ties' of that bourgeois literature which has sold its pen to capital
are today thieves, detectives, prostitutes, pimps, and gangsters.

[...]

We say that socialist realism is the fundamental method of Soviet
fiction and literary criticism, and this implies that revolutionary
romanticism will appear as an integral part of any literary creation, since the whole life of our party, of the working class and its
struggle, is a fusion of the hardest, most matter-of-fact practical
work, with the greatest heroism and vastest perspectives. The
strength of our party has always lain in the fact that it has united
and unites efficiency and practicality with broad vision, with an
incessant forward striving and the struggle to build a communist
society.

*Soviet literature must be able to portray our heroes and to see our tomor-
row. This will not be utopian since our tomorrow is being prepared by
planned and conscious work today.*

[...]

Comrades, the proletariat is the sole heir of the best in the treasure
house of world literature, as in other spheres of material and
world culture. The bourgeoisie has squandered the literary heritage and we much bring it together again carefully, study it and
then, having critically assimilated it, move forward.

[...] Our literature is not yet meeting the demands of our epoch.
The weaknesses in our literature reflect the fact that consciousness
is lagging behind economic life, a state of affairs from which, obvi-
ously, our writers are not exempt. That is why unceasing work on
educating themselves and improving their ideological weapons in
the spirit of socialism are the indispensable conditions without
which Soviet writers cannot change the consciousness of their
readers and thus be engineers of the human soul.

Document 10

Confession

The trial of Iurii Piatakov and sixteen others, held in January
1937, was the second of the three Stalinist show trials. The particular significance of this passage was its establishment of the
supposed 'bloc' between the group of Zinoviev and Kamenev

Selected documents

(tried in August 1936), Piatakov's 'parallel Trotskyist centre', and the 'Rights' under Bukharin and Rykov (tried in March 1938). These people had held diametrically opposed political views in the late 1920s, but had all been part of Lenin's leadership team. Although Piatakov had supported Trotsky in the 1920s he had recanted and held a very responsible post – deputy commissar of heavy industry – until his arrest in September 1936. His trial therefore had more serious implications for other serving members of the Soviet elite than that of a discredited oppositionist like Zinoviev. Before 1930 Bukharin had been a leading Politburo member and Rykov prime minister. The detailed oral confessions made by such senior officials, in open court, gave the charges creditability. The confessions were also undoubtedly intended by Stalin and Ezhov to convince the party elite that it was essential to accelerate the purge process, although in the end many of them were dragged in. Under Gorbachev evidence was produced to show both that such confessions had been achieved by sleep-deprivation, intimidation and beatings, and that Stalin had personally been involved in choosing the final 'version' of the confessions. The verdict against Piatakov, Sokol'nikov and Radek were overturned only in 1988.

From: *Report of the Court Proceedings in the Case of the Anti-Soviet Trotskyist Centre* (Moscow, 1937), pp. 54f.

> *Piatakov*: The characteristic feature of our criminal work in the period from the middle of 1935 to [...] the beginning of 1936 was that this was a period when the 'parallel centre' endeavoured to convert itself [...] into the main centre and to intensify its work in accordance with the directives we had received from Trotsky. [In the prosecution's scenario Piatakov's organisation had been a back-up or 'parallel' centre to the Zinoviev-Kamenev one, which had been broken up after supposedly having organised the assassination of Kirov in December 1934.] [...]
>
> *Vyshinskii* [the prosecutor]: This was the time when Sokol'nikov came to see you and said: ' It is time to begin'? [Sokol'nikov was a co-defendant, who had been a Politburo candidate member in the early 1920s and later deputy commissar for the timber industry].
>
> *Piatakov*: Yes. Just then the new phase began. This was the first

130

conversation in which I told Sokol'nikov what we had, what terrorist groups and Trotskyist organisation we possessed. I told Sokol'nikov, too, in general outline that wrecking activities were being carried out along the lines required. [...]

I remember that during this same conversation much attention was paid to the question of expanding the bloc. Both Sokol'nikov and I knew from Kamenev that the main [Zinoviev-Kamenev] centre had direct and immediate organisational connections with the Rights. On the other hand [...] I had direct contact with Bukharin, which was later maintained by Radek. [Karl Radek was a former Central Committee member who had been a leader of the Comintern.]

Sokol'nikov and I [...] decided that it was absolutely necessary to give form to these relations in some way, so as to organise the work directed towards overthrowing the government in conjunction with the Rights.

We said at the time that it was absolutely necessary to meet one of the leaders of the Rights, i.e. Rykov, Tomskii or Bukharin. [I]n the end the choice fell on Tomskii because we had information that Tomskii had the most numerous and organised cadres and was best fitted to perform such illegal organisational work. [Tomskii had been head of the trade unions until 1930. He shot himself at the time of the Zinoviev-Kamenev trial.]

[...]

[...] In conversation with me, Tomskii told me that he considered it absolutely necessary to organise terrorist and all other kinds of work, but that he would have to consult his comrades, Rykov and Bukharin. This he did later, and then gave me a reply in the name of all three.

Document 11

The great terror: the first 'mass operation'

This extraordinary 'operational order' by Nikolai Ezhov, head of the secret police (NKVD) was only revealed under Gorbachev's glasnost. Although it was issued on 30 July 1937, immediately after the secret trial of Red Army leaders and the expulsion of a number of Stalinist leaders from the party Central Committee, it was ostensibly aimed at non-party elements. It signalled the start of the mass terror. When he fell in 1938 Ezhov was condemned for carrying out indiscriminate 'mass operations' of this type.

Selected documents

From: E. Al'bats, *Mina zamedlennogo deistviia: Politicheskii portret KGB SSSR* [*Delayed Action Mine: Political Portrait of the KGB*] (Moscow, 1992), pp. 319–20, 322–6.

Evidence from the investigation of anti-Soviet groupings is establishing that a significant number of former kulaks, formerly repressed people [*repressirovannye*], escaped prisoners from camps, exile and labour colonies are lying low in the countryside. Lying low are formerly repressed church activists, former active participants of armed anti-Soviet uprisings. A significant number of cadres of anti-Soviet political parties (Socialist-Revolutionaries and [non-Russian nationalists]), and also cadres of former active participants of bandit uprisings, of the Whites, of punitive detachments, of repatriated people, etc., remain almost untouched in the countryside.

Part of those elements enumerated above, moving from the countryside to the towns, have wormed their way into enterprises involved with industry, transport, and construction.

Besides this, significant cadres of criminals – horse thieves, recidivist thieves, looters, etc. having avoided punishment, have made nests in the countryside and the towns, having escaped from prison and hidden from repression. Inadequate struggle with this criminal contingent has created conditions of lawlessness for them, facilitating their criminal activity.

It has been established that all these anti-Soviet elements have been the main instigators of all sorts of anti-Soviet crimes and acts of sabotage, both in the collective and state farms, and in the transport system and in several sectors of industry.

<u>The task of the organs of state security is mercilessly to destroy all this band of anti-Soviet elements, to protect the toiling Soviet people from their counter-revolutionary raids, and once and for all, to finish with their subversive work to undermine the foundations of the Soviet state.</u>

Therefore I Order THE BEGINNING FROM 5 AUGUST 1937 OF AN OPERATION IN ALL REGIONS FOR THE REPRESSION OF FORMER KULAKS, ACTIVE ANTI-SOVIET ELEMENTS, AND CRIMINALS.

[...]

Selected documents

II. On Means of Punishment of Those to be Repressed,
and the Number of Those Subject to Repression

1. All repressed kulak, criminals, and other anti-Soviet elements are to be divided into two categories:

   a) The first category are the most hostile of the enumerated
   elements. They are subject to immediate arrest, and after
   their cases have been considered by a three-person tribunal
   [*troika*] they are TO BE SHOT.

   b) In the second category are the other less active though also
   hostile element. They are subject to arrest and imprisonment in a camp for 8 to 10 years, and the most evil and
   socially dangerous of these, to incarceration for the same
   period in prison, as determined by the three-person tribunal.

2. In accordance with data determined by the peoples commissars of the republics NKVDs and the heads of regional
   administrations of the NKVD, the following numbers of individuals are subject to repression.

	First Category	Second Category	Total
1. Azerbaidzhan SSR	1,500	3,750	5,250
2. Armenian SSR	500	1,000	1,500
3. Belorussian SSR	2,000	10,000	12,000
[...]			
39. Leningrad region	4,000	10,000	14,000
40. Moscow region	5,000	30,000	35,000
[...]			
NKVD camps	10,000	–	10,000
[Total	72,950	177,500	250,450]
[...]			

[III] 1. The operation is to begin on 5 August 1937 and to be complet-
ed in four months.

Document 12

Molotov explains the purges

Viacheslav Molotov, prime minister throughout the 1930s, was
probably Stalin's closest associate. Sacked by Khrushchev from

his main posts in 1957, he was even stripped of party membership under the de-Stalinisation campaign. The poet Feliks Chuev
had a series of interviews with Molotov during his long retire-
ment. Despite the fact that his own wife had been arrested in the
late 1940s, Molotov remained loyal to Stalin's memory. The following extract comes from a conversation of April 1982, when
Molotov was 92.

From: F. I. Chuev, *Sto sorok besed s Molotovym: Iz dnevnika F.
Chueva* [*One Hundred and Forty Conversations with Molotov: From
the Diary of F. Chuev*] (Moscow, 1991), pp. 416f. This fascinating
source is available in English as *Molotov Remembers: Inside
Kremlin Politics: Conversations with Felix Chuev*, ed. Albert Resis,
(Chicago, 1993).

> *Molotov*: The fact of the matter is this: I consider we had to go
> through a period of terror, because we had already been wag-
> ing a struggle for more than ten years. [This presumably refers
> to the long-running conflict in the leadership, which had seen
> the first expulsions of 'oppositionists' from the Politburo in
> 1927.] It cost us dearly, but things would have been worse with-
> out it. Many people suffered who should not have been
> touched. But I believe that Beria on his own could not have
> done it. [Beria actually only took over the secret police at the
> end of 1938, when the purges were winding down; it was
> Beria's predecessor, Ezhov, who is sometimes blamed for the
> purges.] He carried out orders, Stalin's very harsh orders.
>
> *Chuev*: Surely Stalin could never think that we had so many ene-
> mies of the people?
>
> *Molotov*: Of course it is sad and regrettable that there were so
> many such people, but I consider the terror of the late 1930s
> was necessary. Of course, there would have been fewer victims,
> had things been done more cautiously, but Stalin insisted on
> being doubly sure: spare no one, but guarantee a reliable situa-
> tion during the war and after the war, for a long period – and
> that in my opinion was achieved. I do not deny that I support-
> ed that line. I simply could not keep track every individual per-
> son. But people like Bukharin, Rykov, Zinoviev and Kamenev
> were linked with one another. [These men were former
> Politburo members who were victims of the Show trials; one of
> the basic charges of the trials was the 'bloc' between 'rightists'
> like Bukharin and Rykov, and 'leftists' like Zinoviev and

Kamenev; all were Old Bolsheviks. See document 10.]
It was difficult to draw a precise line at which it was possible to stop.

Chuev: They say everything was made up.

Molotov: Look, that is impossible. It was impossible to concoct such a thing. Piatakov [victim of the first 1937 show trial] kept Trotsky informed …

Chuev: They beat them – not everyone could stand it. When some people are beaten, they will write whatever is wanted.

Molotov: Stalin, in my opinion, followed a very correct line: let innocent heads roll, but there will be no wavering during and after the war. There were mistakes. But look, Rokossovskii and Meretskov were freed. [Generals arrested before the war, who subsequently became important wartime commanders.]

Chuev: And how many people like them perished?

Molotov: Not many people like them. I consider that the period of terror was necessary, and it was not possible to carry it through without mistakes. To continue the arguments during the war … If we had we been spineless then …
Vlasov would have been a trifle compared to what might have been. [Vlasov was a Soviet general who was captured by the Germans in 1942 and collaborated with them.] Many people were wavering politically.

Chuev: Could they have gone over to Hitler?

Molotov: Perhaps not, but wavering would have been very dangerous.

Document 13

The Great Fatherland War

Stalin waited nearly two weeks following the German attack to make his first wartime radio address to the Soviet people, on 3 July 1941. The charge that Stalin went into a state of shock at the moment of the attack in now known to be unfounded, but he was badly affected by the collapse of the Western army group in the weeks that followed. This speech endorsed the name by which the Soviet would describe their part of the Second World War, the 'Great Fatherland War'. In a ten-page speech there was only one reference to the Communist party.

Selected documents

From: I. V. Stalin, *Sochineniia*, vol. 2[15], (Stanford, 1967), pp. 1–4, 8–10.

Comrades! Citizens! Brothers and sisters!

Fighting men of the army and navy!

I am making this appeal to you, my friends.

The treacherous attacked by Hitlerite Germany on our mother-land, begun on 22 June, is continuing. [...]

[...]

As to the fact that part of our territory has [...] been occupied by the German-fascist forces, that is mainly explained by the fact that the war [...] was begun under conditions favourable for the German forces and unfavourable for the Soviet forces. The fact is that the German forces [...] were already fully mobilised and the 170 divisions hurled by Germany against the USSR and brought up to the Soviet frontiers were in a state of complete readiness [...] while Soviet forces had still to be mobilised and moved up to the frontiers. It is also of no little importance that fascist Germany suddenly and treacherously violated the non-aggression pact signed in 1939 between it and the USSR [...]

It may be asked: how could the Soviet Government have consent-ed to conclude a non-aggression pact with such treacherous peo-ple and monsters as Hitler and Ribbentrop? Was this not a mistake on the part of the Soviet Government? Of course not! A non-aggression pact is a pact of peace between two states. It was just such a pact that Germany proposed to us in 1939. Could the Soviet Government have declined such a proposal? [...]

What did we gain by concluding with Germany the non-aggres-sion pact? We secured for our country peace for a year and a half and the opportunity of preparing our forces to repulse fascist Germany should it risk an attack on our country despite the pact. [...]

[...]

This war with fascist Germany cannot be considered an ordinary war. It is not only a war between two armies. It is also a great war of the entire Soviet people against the German fascist forces. The aim of this national fatherland war against the Fascist oppressors is not only the elimination of the danger hanging over our coun-try, but also aid to all European peoples groaning under the yoke of German fascism. In this war of liberation we shall not be alone. In this great war we shall have loyal allies in the peoples of Europe and America. [...] This will be a united front of peoples standing for freedom and against enslavement [...] on the part of Hitler's fascist armies. In this connection, the historic speech of the British Prime Minister, Mr. Churchill, regarding aid to the Soviet Union, and the declaration of the United States government of its readiness to render help to our country, which can only evoke a feeling of gratitude in the hearts of the peoples of the Soviet Union, are wholly understandable and significant.

[...]

With the aim of the rapid mobilisation of the all the strength of the peoples of the USSR [...] a State Committee of Defence [GKO] has been created, in whose hands are now concentrated all state power. The State Committee of Defence had begun its work and calls all the people to rally around the party of Lenin and Stalin, around the Soviet Government, for the selfless support of the Red Army and Red Navy, for the defeat of the enemy, for victory.

Document 14

Not one step back!

Stalin's 'Order of the People's Commissar of Defence', no. 227, was issued on 28 July 1942 when the Red Army was suffering a series of defeats on the southern part of the front. The strategic city of Rostov-on-Don has just fallen and the Germans were advancing towards Stalingrad and the Caucasus.

From: *Voenno-istoricheskii zhurnal* [*Military-Historical Journal*] 1988, no. 8, pp. 74f.

[I]t is necessary to completely end any talk to the effect that we can keep on retreating indefinitely, that we have much territory, our country is vast and rich, our population is large, grain will always be abundant. Such talk is false and harmful, it weakens us and strengthens the enemy, for unless we stop retreating we will be without grain, without fuel, without metal, without raw materials, without factories, without railways.

This means it is time to stop retreating.

Not one step back! This must now be our main slogan.

It is necessary steadfastly, to the last drop of blood, to defend each position, each metre of Soviet territory, to hold every patch of Soviet soil, and to hold it as long as possible.

[...]

[O]ur factories in the rear are now working very well and the front is receiving more and more aircraft, tanks, artillery, and mortars.

What don't we have enough of?

We haven't enough order and discipline in our companies, battalions, regiments, divisions, tank units, and air force squadrons. This is now out main shortcoming. We must establish in our army the strictest order and iron discipline, if we want to save the situation and hold our Motherland.

[...]

Commanders of companies, battalions, regiments, divisions, corresponding commissars and political workers, who retreat from combat positions without orders from above are traitors to the Motherland.

[...]

The Supreme Commander of the Red Army orders:

1. The military councils of the army groups [an 'army group' (*front*) was made up of several armies], and especially the commanders of the army groups are:

    a) unconditionally to liquidate the mood of retreat [...]

    b) unconditionally to remove and to send to Supreme Headquarters for commitment to military tribunal commanders of armies allowing retreat and giving up positions without order by the army group command.

    c) To form within the army group from one to three punitive battalions [*shtrafnye batal'ony*] [...] (with 800 men in each), to which are to be sent middle-level and senior commanders and comparable political workers [...] who have been found guilty of breaking discipline by cowardice and lack of firmness, and to despatch them to the most dangerous sectors of the front so that they can be given the chance to make reparation with their blood for their crimes against the Motherland.

2. The military councils of armies and especially the commanders of armies are:

Selected documents

[...]

b) to form within the army three to five well-armed blocking detachments [*zagraditel'nye otriady*] (with up to 200 men in each), to station them in the immediate rear of unsteady divisions and to order them, in the event of panic and disorderly retreat by parts of the division, to shoot on the spot cowards and those who panic and by this means to help those honest fighters of the divisions to fulfil their duty towards the Motherland.

Document 15

Stalin's election speech, 1946

This speech has been frequently cited in the main text. It was made at the time of the (one-candidate) 'election' campaign to the Supreme Soviet. Stalin's public statements were rare after the war, and this was the only time he attempted to give an overview of the mature Stalinist system. It was also seen both within the USSR and abroad as a re-affirmation of the importance of ideology, and as such played its part in the unfolding of the Cold War.

From: I. V. Stalin, *Sochineniia*, vol. 3[16] (Stanford, 1967), pp. 2, 4–5, 19–20.

It would be wrong to believe that the Second World War came about accidentally or as a result of the mistakes of some statesman or other, though mistakes certainly took place. In reality the war came about as the inevitable result of the development of the world economic and political forces on the basis of modern monopoly capitalism. [...]

The fact of the matter is that the unevenness of the development of capitalist countries usually results [...] in an abrupt disruption of the equilibrium within the world system of capitalism, and that a group of capitalist countries which believes itself to be less supplied with raw materials and markets usually makes attempts to alter the situation [...] by means of armed force.

[...]

[...] The war set something in the nature of an examination for our Soviet system, our government, our state, our Communist party, and summed up the results of their work as if telling us: here they are, your people and organisations, their deeds and days [...]

[...]

[...] At another time it would have been necessary to study the speeches and reports of the party's representatives, to analyse them, compare their words with their deeds, sum up results and so forth. [...] Matters are different now that the [...] war itself has checked the work of our organisations and leaders and summed up its results. [...]

[...]

As to plans for a longer period, our party intends to organise a new powerful upsurge of the economy which will give us the possibility, for instance, to treble the level of our industry three-fold as compared with the pre-war level. We must achieve a situation in which out industry is able to produce annually up to 50 million tons of cast iron (*prolonged applause*), up to 60 million tons of steel (*prolonged applause*), up to 500 million tons of coal (*prolonged applause*), up to 60 millions tons of oil (*prolonged applause*). Only under such conditions can we regard our country as guaranteed against any accidents (*stormy applause*). This will require perhaps three new Five-year plans if not more. But this task can be done, and we must do it (*stormy applause*). [...]

Document 16

The Zhdanovshchina

The post-war period saw a campaign to ensure party domination of the arts and the creative intelligentsia. It began with a Central Committee decree of 21 August 1946 on the Leningrad literary journals *Zvezda* and *Leningrad*. The spokesman for this party revival was Stalin's chief ideologist, Andrei Zhdanov, and the period is sometimes called the *Zhdanovshchina* (the reign of Zhdanov). The two passages below deal with a range of cultural activities and reflect the doctine of socialist realism (see document 9) as it have evolved under the influence of the wartime and earl Cold War developments.

From: A. A. Zhdanov, *On Literature, Music and Philosophy*, (London, 1950), pp. 47f, 59, 64–6.

Selected documents

A. Literature. Zhdanov, 'Report on the Journals *Zvezda* and *Leningrad*', August 1946.

However fine may be the external appearance of the work of the fashionable modern bourgeois writers in America and Western Europe, and of their film directors and theatrical producers, they can neither save nor better their bourgeois culture, for its moral basis is rotten and decaying. [...] A swarm of bourgeois writers, film directors, and theatrical producers are trying to draw the attention of the progressive strata of society away from the acute problems of social and political struggle and to divert it into a groove of cheap meaningless art and literature, treating with gangsters and show-girls and glorifying the adulterer and the adventures of crooks and gamblers.

Is this fitting for us Soviet patriots, the representatives of advanced Soviet culture, to play the part of admirers or disciples of bourgeois culture? Our literature, reflecting an order on a higher level than any bourgeois-democratic order and a culture manifoldly superior to bourgeois culture, has, it goes without saying, the right to teach the new universal morals to others.

Where is another such people or country as ours to be found? Where are such splendid qualities to found as our Soviet people displayed in the Great Patriotic War and are displaying every day in the labour of converting our economy to peaceful development and material and cultural rehabilitation.

B. Music and art. Zhdanov's concluding speech at a conference of Soviet 'music workers', January 1948.

[O]ur formalists, undermining the foundations of true music, compose music which is ugly and false, permeated with idealist sentiment, alien to the broad masses of the people, and created not for the millions of Soviet people, but for chosen individuals and small groups, for an elite. How unlike Glinka, Tchaikovsky Rimsky-Korsakov, Dargomyzhskii, Mussorgsky [the great nineteenth-century Russian classical composers], who considered the basis for development of their creative power to be the ability to express in their works the spirit of the people. By ignoring the wants of the people and its spirit and creative genius, the formalist trend in music has clearly demonstrated its anti-popular character.

[...]

[I]nnovation does not always imply progress. Many young musicians are being confused by being told that unless they are original they are not new and would become imprisoned in conserva-

141

tive traditions. Since, however, innovation is not synonymous with progress, the spreading of ideas of this sort means gross delusion, if not deceit. Furthermore, the 'innovations' of the formalists are not new at all, since their 'novelty' brings to mind contemporary decadent bourgeois music of Europe and America. This is where we should look for the real 'epigones' [i.e. imitators].

You will remember that at one time [in the 1920s] in all primary and secondary schools there was a passion for 'experimental' methods […] according to which the part of the teacher was reduced to a minimum and every pupil had the right to decide upon the subject of a lesson. […]

This was called an 'experimental' method, but meant in fact that the whole organisation of study went topsy-turvy. […]

We know that the party abolished these 'innovations'. Why? Because, although very 'left' in form, there were reactionary through and through and were leading to a nullification of the school.

Take another example. […] As you know, at one time there were strong bourgeois influences at work in painting which came to the surface now and again under extremely 'left' flags and attached to themselves names like futurism, cubism, and modernism. Under the slogan of 'Overthrow rotten academism' they called for innovation, and this innovation reached its most insane point when a girl, for instance, would be portrayed with one head and forty legs, one eye looking at you and the other at the North Pole.

How did it all end? With a complete fiasco of the new trend. The Party fully re-established the significance of the classical heritage of Repin, Briullov, Vereshchagin, Vasnetsov, and Surikov [nineteenth-century Russian realist painters]. Did we act correctly when we defended the treasure-house of classical painting and destroyed the liquidators of painting? […]

Thus it is in music, too. We do not assert that the classical heritage represents the absolute peak of musical culture. If we said that it would be tantamount to admitting that progress came to an end with the classics. Up to now, however, the classics remain unsurpassed. […]

[T]o give frank expression to what goes on in the minds of a Soviet audience one would have to say that it would do no harm if more compositions appeared amongst us which approached classical music with regard to content, form, polish, and beauty of melody.

Document 17

The two camps

The founding conference of the Communist Information Bureau, the Cominform, took place in Poland in September 1947. Zhdanov made more ideological pronouncements here, this time on foreign policy ideology. The concept of the 'two camps' (*dva lageria*), however, was based on Lenin and Stalin's writings from the civil war period; it is another example of the militarised Soviet vocabulary (and *lager'*, of course, had an additional Stalinist usage – as in the GULAG). The creation of the Cominform was the Soviet response to two American initiatives, the Truman Doctrine, which provided military aid to the Greek and Turkish governments, and the Marshall Plan, which offered aid to a range of European countries. The Cominform was disbanded in 1956, the same year the USSR's foreign policy doctrine changed from 'two camps' to 'peaceful coexistence'.

From: G. Procaccci (ed.), *The Cominform: Minutes of the Three Conferences* (Milan, 1994), pp. 247–9, 457–9.

In the post-war period sharp changes have taken place in the international situation. [...] Two opposite political lines took shape: at one pole, the policy of the USSR and the democratic countries, aimed at undermining imperialism and strengthening democracy; at the other pole the policy of the USA and Britain, aimed at strengthening imperialism and strangling democracy. Since the USSR and the countries of the new democracy [i.e. the Eastern European communist governments] have become a hindrance to the realisation of the imperialist plans of struggle for world domination and the defeat of the democratic movements, a campaign has been proclaimed against the USSR and the countries of the new democracy, reinforced by threats of a new war on the part of the most ardent imperialist politicians in the USA and Britain.

Thus two camps have come into being [...]

The struggle between the two opposed camps [...] is taking place in circumstances of further aggravation of the general crisis of capitalism, weakening of the capitalist forces and strengthening of the forces of socialism and democracy.

Consequently, the imperialist camp and its leading force, the USA, are displaying particularly frenzied activity. The Truman-Marshall Plan is only one component part […] of a general plan of world-wide expansionist policy that is being carried out by the USA in all parts of the world. […] Yesterday's aggressors, the capitalist magnates of Germany and Japan, are being groomed by America for a new role, that of serving as an instrument of the USA's imperialist policy in Europe and Asia.

[…]

Under these conditions it is essential for the anti-imperialist and democratic camp to close ranks, work out a common programme of actions and develop its own tactics against the main forces of the imperialist camp, against American imperialism, against its British and French allies, and against the right-wing socialists, in the first place those in Britain and France. [There was a Labour government in Britain at this time, and in France anti-Communist socialists were prominent.]

[…]

The dissolution of the Comintern […] has played its positive role. [The Comintern, or 3rd International, was created in 1919 and disbanded in 1943.] The dissolution of the Comintern has forever put an end to the slanders of the enemies of communism and the labour movement to the effect that Moscow allegedly interferes in the internal life of other states and that the Communist parties of the various countries allegedly act not in the interests of their own peoples but on orders from abroad.

[…]

In the present situation, however, there are also shortcomings in the Communist parties. Some comrades understood the dissolution of the Comintern as meaning the liquidation of all links […] Yet experience has shown that such disconnection between Communist parties is incorrect, harmful, and essentially unnatural.

Document 18

Stalin and the Korean war

A. Excerpts from a telegram of 30 January 1950 from Stalin to Shtykov, Soviet ambassador in North Korea. Publication of this document first confirmed Stalin's direct involvement in the start of the Korean War in June 1950, although this involvement has

since been made clearer by other material. There is some dis-
agreement as to whether Stalin was simply responding to desire
of Kim Il Sung, the North Korean communist leader, for an invasion of the South or whether he put him Kim up to it.

From: Kathryn Weathersby, 'Korea, 1949–50', *Cold War
International History Project Bulletin*, 5 (1995), 9.

> 1. I received your report. [In a telegram of 19 January ambassador
> Shtykov reported Kim's request for permission to launch a con-
> ventional attack on the South in order to to unify Korea.] I under-
> stand the dissatisfaction of Comrade Kim Il Sung, but he must
> understand that such a large matter in regard to South Korea such
> as he wants to undertake needs large preparation. The matter
> must be organised so that there would not be too great a risk. If he
> wants to discuss this matter with me, then I will always be ready
> to receive him and discuss with him. Transmit all this to Kim Il
> Sung and tell him that I am ready to help him in this matter.
>
> 2. I have a request for Comrade Kim Il Sung. The Soviet Union is
> experiencing a great insufficiency in lead. We would like to receive
> from Korea a yearly minimum of 25 thousand tons of lead. [...]
> Transmit this request of mine to comrade Kim Il Sung and ask him
> for me, to communicate to me his consideration on this matter.

B. Excerpts from a telegram from Stalin to Mao Zedong, October
1950. The June North Korean invasion failed to completely over-
run the South, and after American-led landings behind their
lines in September the North Korean position collapsed.
Communist China (established in 1949) eventually intervened
with troops to stabilise the Communist front, but only after
major disagreements with the USSR over whether Moscow
would provide air cover. Stalin's letter to Mao, included in a letter to Kim Il Sung of 8 October 1950 – and written under the nom
de guerre Fyn Si – perhaps reveals much about the Soviet
leader's general attitude to the Cold War.

From: A. Y. Mansourov, 'Stalin, Mao, Kim, and China's Decision
[...]', *Cold War International History Project Bulletin*, 6–7 (1995–96),
116.

> [...] While raising before You the question of despatching
> [Chinese] troops to Korea, I considered 5–6 divisions a minimum,

not a maximum, and I was proceeding from the following consid-
erations of an international character:

[...] The USA, as the Korean events showed, is not ready at present for a big war;

[...]

[...] The USA will be compelled to yield in the Korean question to
China, behind which stands its ally, the USSR, and will have to
agree to such terms of settlement of the Korean question that
would be favourable to Korea and would not give the enemies a
possibility to transform Korea into their springboard;

[...]

Of course, I took into account also [the possibility] that the USA,
despite its unreadiness for a big war, could still be drawn into a
big war out of [considerations of] prestige, which, in turn, would
drag China into the war, and along with this draw into the war the
USSR, which is bound with China by the Mutual Assistance Pact
[i.e. the Sino-Soviet treaty of 1950]. Should we fear this? In my
opinion, we should not, because together we will be stronger than
the USA and England, while the other European capitalist states
[...] do not present serious military forces. If a war in inevitable,
then let it be waged now, and not in a few years when Japanese
militarism will be restored as an ally of the USA and when the
USA and Japan will have a ready-made bridgehead on the conti-
nent in a form of the entire Korea run by Syngman Rhee [the South
Korean leader].

Document 19

Stalin is our history

The following exchange took part during a pause at a Politburo
meeting in July 1984, just before the beginning of perestroika.
One of the problems facing Russia in the 1980s was that it was
still run by ageing Stalinists: Chernenko, the party chief, was 73;
Tikhonov, the prime minister, was 79; Ustinov, long associated
with the military-industrial complex, was 76. The old men running the USSR had come to positions of power under Stalin and
clearly still resented the de-Stalinising efforts of Khrushchev a
quarter of a century earlier. Among many other measures
Khrushchev had expelled three of Stalin's closest associates,
Molotov, Kaganovich and Malenkov, from the leadership and

Selected documents

from the party. A cautious note came from Gorbachev, born in 1931 and the representative of a new generation.

From: *Cold War International History Project Bulletin*, 4 (1994), 81.

Tikhonov: In general we did the right thing in restoring [Molotov] to the party. [This had just taken place.]

Chernenko: And right after this the C[entral] C[ommittee] of the CPSU received letters from Malenkov and Kaganovich [...]
Allow me to read Kaganovich's letter. *(Reads the letter.)*
A letter with analogous contents, with a confession of his mistakes, was sent by Malenkov.

Tikhonov: Maybe for now we shouldn't do anything with these letters?

Chernenko: For now we can do nothing, but let's agree to examine them after the 27th Congress of our party.

Ustinov: But in my opinion, Malenkov and Kaganovich should be reaccepted into the party. They were active figures, leaders. I will say, frankly, that if not for Khrushchev, then the decision to expel these people from the party would not have been taken. And in general those scandalous disgraces which Khrushchev committed in relation to Stalin would never have occurred. Stalin, no matter what is said, is our history. No one enemy brought us so much harm as Khrushchev did in his policy towards the past of our party and our state, and towards Stalin.

[...]

Ustinov: [...] In connection with the fortieth anniversary of the Victory over fascism [May 1985] I would propose discussing one more question. Shouldn't we restore the name of Stalingrad to Volgograd? [The city where the famous battle took place was renamed under Khrushchev.] Millions of people would support this. But this, as they say, is information for thought.

Gorbachev: This proposal has positive and negative sides.

Tikhonov: Recently a very good documentary film was released called 'Marshal Zhukov', in which Stalin is portrayed rather fully and positively.

Chernenko: I watched it. This is a good film.

Ustinov: I really should see it.

147

Bibliographical essay

This short selection only includes books and articles in English. It also favours the most recent publications, based as they increasingly are on material obtained directly or indirectly from the Russian archives and on first-hand accounts. The subtitle is included if it makes the work's subject clearer. The order of the bibliography follows the chapter order.

General works

New reflective works on the whole Soviet experience, including the place of the formative Stalin years are: **[1]** R. Daniels, *The End of the Communist Revolution* (New York, 1993), and **[2]** M. Malia, 'To the Stalin mausoleum', in S. Graubard, *Eastern Europe ... Central Europe ... Europe* (Boulder CO, 1991). Of general interpretations I have been most influenced by **[3]** M. Lewin, *The Making of the Soviet System: Essays in the Social History of Interwar Russia* (London, 1985), which is supplemented by his **[4]** *Russia/USSR/Russia* (New York, 1995). Two books by R. W. Davies give the best discussion of new material and re-interpretations coming from the new Russia: **[5]** *Soviet History in the Gorbachev Revolution* (Basingstoke, 1989), and **[6]** *Soviet History in the Yeltsin Era* (Basingstoke, 1997).

[7] G. Boffa, *The Stalin Phenomenon* (Ithaca, 1992), a thoughtful Eurocommunist overview of historians' perspectives, is now dated (the original Italian edition appeared in 1982), but it is still the best introduction. **[8]** C. Ward, *Stalin's Russia* (London, 1993), lays out many of the debates very clearly. Also valuable, although less of a coherent whole, are the essays in **[9]** R. Tucker (ed.), *Stalinism: Essays in Historical Interpretation* (New York, 1977), **[10]** A. Nove (ed.), *The Stalin Phenomenon* (London, 1993), **[11]** J. Cooper *et al.* (eds), *Soviet History, 1917–45* (Basingstoke, 1995), **[12]** I. Kershaw and M. Lewin (eds),

Stalinism and Nazism: Dictatorships in Comparison (Cambridge, 1997), and **[13]** J. Channon (ed.), *Politics, Society and Stalinism in the USSR,* (Basingstoke, 1997).

In terms of primary sources a new English-language version of Stalin's collected writings would be most useful. The thirteen volume editions of **[14]** J. Stalin, *Works* (London, 1952–55), are not easy to obtain, although there were Maoist reprints in the 1960s and 1970s. Also hard to get is **[15]** Bruce Franklin (ed.), *The Essential Stalin* (London, 1973), although that does not in any event go far beyond what is available in contemporary translations of the one-volume selection, *Problems of Leninism* (*Voprosy leninizma*). There is interesting material in **[16]** L. Lih, *et al.* (eds), *Stalin's Letters to Molotov, 1925–1936* (New Haven, 1995), as well as a long and thought-provoking introduction. The best collection of official documentation in English is still **[17]** R. McNeal (ed.), *Resolutions and Decisions of the Communist Party of the Soviet Union* (Toronto, 1974), vol. 3 of which covers the Stalin period. An important primary source, historically significant in its own right, is Khrushchev's 1956 secret speech. It was published in some editions of Stickle (see no. 19) and in **[18]** T. H. Rigby, *The Stalin Dictatorship* (Sydney, 1968); the Rigby edition also contains important de-Stalinising material from the 1961 party congress. Also available in English now is the Soviet elite's discussion of Stalin's later years at the July 1953 Central Committee plenum, **[19]** D. M. Stickle (ed.), *The Beria Affair: The Secret Transcripts of the Meetings Signalling the End of Stalinism* (New York, 1992). Two essential accounts by insiders include **[20]** N. Khrushchev, *Khruschev Remembers,* (London, 1971, 1974), **[21]** *Khruschev Remembers: The Glasnost Tapes* (Boston, 1990), and **[22]** A. Resis (ed.), *Molotov Remembers: Conversations with Felix Chuev* (Chicago, 1993).

On Stalin himself the fullest biographies are provided by **[23]** D. Volkogonov, *Stalin* (London, 1991), and two volumes by R. Tucker, **[24]** *Stalin as Revolutionary, 1879–1929* (London, 1974), and **[25]** *Stalin in Power, 1928–1941* (New York, 1990). Another recent Western account, although like Tucker not benefitting from the glasnost revelations, is **[26]** R. McNeal, *Stalin* (Basingstoke, 1988). New treatments of aspects of Stalin's early career include **[27]** R. Slusser, *Stalin in October* (Baltimore, 1987), and **[28]** Stephen Blank, *The Sorcerer as Apprentice: Stalin as Commissar of Nationalities, 1917–1924* (Westport, 1994).

Politics

The best general analysis is **[29]** G. Gill, *The Origins of the Stalinist Political System* (Cambridge, 1990). For new details of the working of the state there is **[30]** D. Watson, *Molotov and Soviet Government: Sovnarkom, 1930–41* (Basingstoke, 1996). **[31]** O. Khlevniuk, *In Stalin's Shadow: The*

Career of 'Sergo' Ordzhonikidze (Armonk NY, 1995), is a study by an important native specialist. **[32]** C. Merridale, *Moscow Politics and the Rise of Stalin* (Basingstoke, 1990), is an important study of local politics. The post-war years are still inadequately studied, except in the context of the Cold War. See, however, **[33]** W. Hahn, *Postwar Soviet Politics: The Fall of Zhdanov and the Defeat of Moderation, 1946–53* (Ithaca, 1982), and **[34]** T. Dunmore, *Soviet Politics 1945–53* (Basingstoke, 1984). In the command economy the boundary between politics and economics was extremely ill-defined, and there is much that is 'political' in the following sections.

The economy

As a general introduction **[35]** A. Nove, *An Economic History of the USSR, 1971–1991* (London, 1992), is still useful, although the first edition dates back to 1962. As background there is now **[36]** P. Gregory, *Before Command: An Economic History or Russia from Emancipation to the First Five Year Plan* (Princeton, 1995). **[37]** R. W. Davies *et al.* (eds), *The Economic Transformation of the Soviet Union, 1913–1945* (Cambridge, 1994) is invaluable as an overview for the first two periods of the Stalinist economy.

The definitive English-language work on Stalin's economic policies in the pivotal late 1920s and early 1930s is the series now edited by R. W. Davies and entitled *The Industrialisation of Soviet Russia*. This is the continuation of E. H. Carr's series, *The Bolshevik Revolution, 1917–1923*, *The Interregnum, 1923–1924, Socialism in One Country, 1924–1926*, and *Foundations of a Planned Economy, 1926–1929*. Agriculture is covered in vols. 1, 2, and 5 of *The Industrialisation of Soviet Russia*: **[38]** *The Socialist Offensive: The Collectivisation of Soviet Agriculture, 1929–1930* (London, 1980), **[39]** *The Soviet Collective Farm, 1929–1930* (London, 1980) and the forthcoming [40] *The Years of Hunger: Soviet Agriculture and the Famine, 1931–1933* (with S. Wheatcroft). For industry the relevant volumes (3 and 4) are **[41]** *The Soviet Economy in Turmoil, 1929–1930* (Basingstoke, 1989), and **[42]** *Crisis and Progress in the Soviet Economy, 1931–1933* (Basingstoke, 1996). A related work involving some of those working with Davies at Birmingham University is **[43]** E. Rees (ed.), *Decision-Making in the Stalinist Command Economy, 1932–1937* (Basingstoke, 1997). **[44]** H. Hunter and J. Szymer, *Faulty Foundations: Soviet Economic Policies, 1928–1940* (Princeton, 1992), uses complicated techniques to make clear and important points.

Stalinist agriculture is dealt with in a number of specialist works. **[45]** M. Lewin, *Russian Peasants and Soviet Power* (London, 1968), is still one of the most important studies of collectivization. Also relevant here are two volumes by J. Hughes, **[46]** *Stalin, Siberia and the Crisis of the New*

Economic Policy (Cambridge, 1991), and **[47]** *Stalinism in a Russian Province: Collectivization and Dekulakization in Siberia* (Basingstoke, 1995). On wartime food supply see **[48]** W. Moskoff, *The Bread of Affliction* (Cambridge, 1990).

Society

Good surveys of the early changes are **[49]** V. Andrle, *A Social History of Twentieth-Century Russia* (London, 1994), and **[50]** S. Fitzpatrick, *The Russian Revolution* (Oxford, 1994). **[51]** W. Rosenberg and L. Siegelbaum (eds), *The Social Dimensions of Soviet Industrialization* (Bloomington IN, 1993), is an important collection of essays. See also **[52]** R. Thurston, *Life and Terror in Stalin's Russia, 1934–1941* (New Haven CT, 1996). There is still little on social history after 1941, but a beginning has been made in **[53]** J. Barber and M. Harrison, *The Soviet Home Front 1941–1945* (Harlow, 1991), and **[54]** S. Fitzpatrick, 'Postwar Soviet society: the "return to normalcy", 1945–1953' in S. Linz, *The Impact of World War II on the Soviet Union* (Totowa NJ, 1985).

For the social history of the village see also the works already cited on the agrarian economy, and **[55]** R. Conquest, *Harvest of Sorrow* (London, 1986), which is especially strong on the Ukrainian famine. The latest overviews are **[56]** S. Fitzpatrick, *Stalin's Peasants: Resistance and Survival in the Russian Village after Collectivization* (Oxford, 1995). **[57]** L. Viola, *Peasant Rebels under Stalin: Collectivisation and the Culture of Peasant Resistance* (New York, 1996). The history of the Stalinist working class in the 1930s was a major focus of the revisionists of the 1980s, even before the onset of glasnost: **[58]** D. Filtzer, *Soviet Workers and Stalinist Industrialization* (London, 1986), **[59]** H. Kuromiya, *Stalin's Industrial Revolution* (Cambridge, 1988), **[60]** V. Andrle, *Workers in Stalin's Russia* (Hemel Hempstead, 1988), **[61]** L. Siegelbaum, *Stakhanovism and the Politics of Productivity in the USSR, 1935–1941* (Cambridge, 1988). For an introduction to more recent work see the essays in **[62]** L. Siegelbaum and R. Suny (eds), *Making the Workers Soviet* (Ithaca, 1994). Grass-roots case studies of urbanisation are **[63]** E. Hoffmann, *Peasant Metropolis: Social Identities in Moscow, 1929–1941* (Ithaca, 1994), and **[64]** S. Kotkin, *Magnetic Mountain* (Berkeley, 1995); the latter draws broad conclusions based on the steel town of Magnitogorsk. Another kind of worker-peasant interaction was dealt with in **[65]** L. Viola, *The Best Sons of the Fatherland: Workers in the Vanguard of Soviet Collectivization* (Oxford, 1987). On women and the family there is **[66]** W. Goldman, *Women, the State and Revolution: Family Policy and Social Life, 1917–1936* (Cambridge, 1993). **[67]** S. Fitzpatrick, *Education and Social Mobility in the Soviet Union, 1921–1934* (Cambridge, 1979), has, along with her later articles, been very influential in the history of the intelligentsia.

151

Culture

There are useful articles in **[68]** H. Günther (ed.), *The Culture of the Stalin Period* (Basingstoke, 1990), and in **[69]** S. Fitzpatrick, *The Cultural Front: Power and Culture in Revolutionary Russia* (Ithaca, 1992). For an outline of Russian literature see **[70]** E. Brown, *Russian Literature since the Revolution* (Cambridge MA, 1982). Three interpretative works with special insights in Stalinism and Socialist Realism are **[71]** V. Dunham, *In Stalin's Time: Middleclass Values in Soviet Fiction* (Durham, 1990), **[72]** K. Clark, *The Soviet Novel* (Chicago, 1985), and **[73]** R. Robin, *Socialist Realism* (Palo Alto, 1992). The 1930s policy towards writers (and indirectly other members of the creative intelligentsia) is covered by **[74]** A. Kemp-Welch, *Stalin and the Literary Intelligentsia, 1928–1939* (London, 1991). Extraordinary archival material on repression of writers appears in **[75]** V. Shentalinsky, *The KGB's Literary Archive* (London, 1995). **[76]** R. Taylor and D. Spring (eds), *Stalinism and Soviet Cinema* (New York, 1993), covers various aspects of film. For painting and sculpture there are **[77]** I. Golomstock, *Totalitarian Art in the Soviet Union, the Third Reich, Fascist Italy and the People's Republic of China* (London, 1990), and **[78]** M. Bown, *Art under Stalin* (Oxford, 1991). The published catalogues to two recent exhibitions are well illustrated and have extensive background text: **[79]** M. Bown, *Soviet Socialist Realist Painting* (Oxford, 1992), and **[80]** D. Ades *et al.*, *Art and Power: Europe under the Dictators 1930–45* (London, 1995). On architecture and town planning see **[81]** A. Tarkhanov and S. Kavtaradze, *Stalinist Architecture* (London, 1992).

The expanding literature on popular culture includes **[82]** R. Stites, *Russian Popular Culture: Entertainment and Society since 1900* (Cambridge, 1992), and **[83]** R. Stites (ed.), *Culture and Entertainment in Wartime Russia* (Bloomington IN, 1995). An excellent anthology is **[84]** J. von Geldern, and R. Stites (eds), *Mass Culture in Soviet Russia* (Bloomington IN, 1995). **[85]** R. Edelman, *Serious Fun: A History of Spectator Sports in the USSR* (New York, 1993), deals with an area that is frequently ignored.

The nationalities

The most stimulating recent overview is **[86]** R. Suny, *The Revenge of the Past: Nationalism, Revolution, and the Collapse of the Soviet Union* (Stanford, 1993). A solid survey of events is **[87]** G. Simon, *Nationalism and Policy toward the Nationalities in the Soviet Union* (Boulder CO, 1991). Although much more information has appeared in Russian since 1988, the standard English-language works on the Stalinist deportations are still **[88]** R. Conquest, *The Nation Killers. The Soviet Deportation of Nationalities* (London, 1970), and **[89]** A. Nekrich, *The Punished Peoples: The Deportation and Fate of Soviet Minorities at the End of the Second World*

War (New York, 1978). Two recent works deal in more detail with the largest of the minorities: **[90]** G. Liber, *Soviet Nationality Policy, Urban Growth, and Identity Change in the Ukrainian SSR, 1923–1934* (New York, 1992), and **[91]** D. Marples, *Stalinism in Ukraine in the 1940s* (New York, 1992).

Foreign relations and the war

The standard works for the pre-war period are still the three volumes by J. Haslam: **[92]** *Soviet Foreign Policy, 1930–1933* (London, 1983), **[93]** *The Soviet Union and the Struggle for Collective Security in Europe, 1933–39* (London, 1984), and **[94]** *The Soviet Union and the Threat from the East, 1933-1941* (London, 1992). For a good short introduction see **[95]** T Uldricks, 'Soviet security policy in the 1930s' and other articles in G. Gorodetsky (ed.), *Soviet Foreign Policy, 1917–1991* (London, 1994). Uldricks also provided an excellent overview of the 1920s in **[96]** 'Russia and Europe', *International History Review*, 1:1 (1979), 55–83. New material is incorporated in **[97]** G. Roberts, *The Soviet Union and the Origins of the Second World War* (Basingstoke, 1995). **[98]** K. McDermott and J. Agnew, *The Comintern* (Basingstoke, 1996), is the latest account about Moscow's international.

The most comprehensive treatment of wartime policy is **[99]** V. Mastny, *Russia's Road to the Cold War* (New York, 1979); the post-war sequel is his **[100]** *The Cold War and Soviet Insecurity* (New York, 1997). The view that Stalin's pre-war foreign policy was expansionist is developed by **[101]** R. Raack, *Stalin's Drive to the West 1938–45* (Cambridge, 1995). Soviet policy in the Cold War proper has attracted intense interest. Influential early works, attempting to work out the dynamics of policy formation include: **[102]** M. Shulman, *Stalin's Foreign Policy Reappraised* (Cambridge, 1963), **[103]** W. McCagg, *Stalin Embattled: 1943–1948* (Detroit, 1978), **[104]** W. Taubman, *Stalin's American Policy* (New York, 1982), and **[105]** G. Ra'anan, *International Policy Formation in the USSR: Factional 'Debates' during the Zhdanovshchina* (Hamden CN, 1984); As well as its inherent importance a very useful survey of the literature is contained in **[106]** D. Holloway, *Stalin and the Bomb* (New Haven, 1994). **[107]** V. Zubok and C. Pleshakov, *Inside the Kremlin's Cold War* (Cambridge MA, 1996) represents a new generation of Russian research based on archives and documentary publications. The developing situation is Asia is covered by **[108]** S. Goncharov and J. Lewis, *Uncertain Partners: Stalin, Mao, and the Korean War* (Stanford, 1993). For the ideological dimension see the introductory articles to **[109]** G. Procacci *et al.* (eds), *The Cominform* (Milan, 1994), and **[110]** R. Day, *Cold War Capitalism: The View from Moscow, 1945-1975* (Armonk NJ, 1995). On a key area of European Cold War policy there is **[111]** N. Naimark, *The*

Russians in Germany: A History of the Soviet Zone of Occupation, 1945–49 (Cambridge MA, 1996). On early strategic policy, in addition to no. 106, see **[112]** S. Zaloga, *Target America: The Soviet Union and the Strategic Arms Race, 1945–1964* (Novato CA, 1993).

The best short account of the war is now: **[113]** D. Glantz and J. House, *When Titans Clashed* (Lawrence KA, 1995). Fuller information, also mainly from Russian sources are the classic works of John Erickson: **[114]** *The Road to Stalingrad* (New York, 1975); and **[115]** *The Road to Berlin* (Boulder, 1983). Two important collection of post-glasnost articles are; **[116]** J. Erickson and D. Dilks (eds), *Barbarossa* (Edinburgh, 1994); and **[117]** J. Wieszynski (ed.), *Operation Barbarossa* (Salt Lake City, 1993). **[118]** H Shukman, *Stalin's Generals* (London, 1993) is a collection of new biographies and supplements the excellent collection of military memoirs in **[119]** S. Bialer, *Stalin and his Generals* (New York, 1966). The prewar armed forces purges were dealt with in a samizdat (unofficial) account in **[120]** V. Rapoport and Yuri Alexeev, *High Treason: Essays on the History of the Red Army, 1918–1938* (Durham NC, 1985). For a revisionist account, based on new sources see **[121]** R. Reese, *Stalin's Reluctant Soldiers* (Lawrence KA, 1996). The notion of a planned Soviet offensive war is developed in **[122]** V. Suvorov [V. Rezun], *Icebreaker: Who Started the Second World War?* (London, 1990), and **[123]** E. Topitsch, *Stalin's War: A Radical New Theory on the Origins of the Second World War* (London, 1987). On the extraordinary 'cult' of the war see **[124]** N. Tumarkin, *The Living and the Dead* (New York, 1994).

Terror

The major accounts of Stalin's period in power deal in detail with the purges, especially nos. 23 and 24 (Volkogonov and Tucker). Two standard narratives of Terror, still useful, are **[125]** R. Conquest, *The Great Terror: A Reassessment* (Oxford, 1990; 1st ed., 1965), and **[126]** R. Medvedev, *Let History Judge* (New York, 1989; 1st ed. c. 1972). Conquest also produced a new survey of the Kirov murder, **[127]** *Stalin and the Kirov Assassination* (New York, 1989). The landmark revisionist re-interpretation is **[128]** J. A. Getty, *The Origins of the Great Purges: The Soviet Communist Party Reconsidered, 1933–1938* (Cambridge, 1985). **[129]** J. A. Getty and R. T. Manning (eds), *Stalinist Terror: New Perspectives* (Cambridge, 1993), and **[130]** A. Nove (ed.), *The Stalin Phenomenon* (London, 1993) are collections of essays based partly on new historical material; see also no. 52 (Thurston). The article by O. Khlevniuk, 'The objectives of the Great Terror, 1937–38' in no. 11 (Cooper), pp. 158–176, is especially important, as he has written a number of the important Russian language monographs on the subject. Two new surveys of the archival findings on the numbers of victims of the Terror see **[131]** J. A.

Getty *et al.*, 'Victims of the Soviet penal system in the pre-war years', *American Historical Review*, 98:4 (1993), 1017–49, and **[132]** S. Wheatcroft, 'The scale of German and Soviet repression and mass killings, 1930–45', *Europe-Asia Studies*, 48:8 (1996), 1319–1355. The post-1938 purges are comprehensively dealt with in **[133]** M. Parrish, *The Lesser Terror: Soviet State Security, 1939–1953* (Westport CO, 1996), and in **[134]** A. Knight, *Beria* (Princeton, 1993). The anti-Jewish campaign is now well documented in **[135]** L. Rapoport, *Stalin's War against the Jews: The Doctors' Plot and the Soviet Solution* (New York, 1990).

On the secret police see especially **[136]** R. Conquest, *Inside Stalin's Secret Police: NKVD Politics, 1936–39* (London, 1985), and for the later period nos. 133 and 134 (Parrish and Knight). Accounts of the labour camp system include the famous **[137]** A. Solzhenitsyn, *The GULAG Archipelago* (London, 1974–78). On wartime developments see **[138]** E. Bacon, *The GULAG at War: Stalin's Forced Labour System in the Light of the Archives* (Basingstoke, 1994). Two classic accounts of life in the GULAG are Solzhenitsyn's novella **[139]** *One Day in the Life of Ivan Denisovich* (New York, 1963) and the memoir by E. Ginzburg **[140]**, *Into the Whirlwind* (New York, 1967).

Periodicals

Periodicals continue to provide the cutting edge of work on the Stalin years. In North America there are *Slavic Review* and *Russian Review*; much has also appeared about the post-war period in the *Cold War International History Project Bulletin*. The British *Europe-Asia Studies* (formerly *Soviet Studies*) and the more specialised *Journal of Slavic* (formerly Soviet) *Military Studies* contain much of interest. Work by Russian scholars appears in translation in *Russian Studies in History* (formerly *Soviet Studies in History*).

Index

Index

Riutin platform, 101, 124–7
Rokossovskii, K. K., 135
Romania, 82
Russian Association of Proletarian Writers (RAPP), 55, 127–8
Russian nationalism, 30, 58, 73, 83, 88, 111, 123–4
Rykov, A. I., 22, 104, 130, 134

Second World War, 84–95
food supply, 37
German occupation policy, 91
human losses, 43–4, 84, 88–9, 93–4
and nationalism, 73
and peasants, 46
prisoners of war, 91, 106
surprise attack (1941), 87, 136
war industry, 28–9, 33–4
secretariat (of Communist party), 18, 23
secret police, 15, 69–70, 88, 99, 104, 107, 109, 126, 131–3
Shakhty trial (1928), 55
Short Course (party history), 6, 42
Shostakovich, D. D., 58
show trials see terror
Sino–Soviet treaty (1950), 146
Smersh, 107
Smolensk, Battle of (1941), 89
social history approach, 3
socialism in one country see Stalin, I. V.
socialist realism, 56, 129
Sokol'nikov, G. Ia., 130–1
Solzhenitsyn, A. I., 4, 99
Soviet–Finnish War (1939–40), 86
Sovnarkom see Council of People's Commissars
Spanish Civil War, 78, 86
special settlements see terrror
Stalin, I. V.
and Allied leaders, 78

and Bolshevik revolution, 117
brothers and sisters speech (1941), 89, 135–7
and collectivisation, 36, 38, 122–3
cult of personality, 22, 57, 59
and culture, 22, 56–7, 59, 127–8
death, 108
declining health, 24–5, 108
election speech (1946), 15, 28–31, 39, 62, 77, 83, 94, 113, 139–40
evaluation of United States, 146
family, 12
and foreign policy, 80, 83
and intensification of class struggle, 104, 120
and Kirov assassination, 102–3
and Korean war, 144–6
Marxism and the national question, 64
and nationalities policy, 63–4, 67, 74
Not one step back! order, 87, 137–9
overall assessment, 114
personal qualities, 12–13, 114
pre-revolutionary career, 7, 10–13, 16
re-evaluation by 1980s leaders, 147
and Riutin platform, 125
role in terror, 101, 104–5, 108–9, 111, 130
secretariat as source of power, 18
socialism in one country, 10, 117–19
and specialists, 119–20
speech to economic managers (1931), 30, 123–4
and threat of war, 87
victory in succession struggle, 21–3

161